BIOCULTURAL EVOLUTION

a workbook for
physical anthropology
and archaeology

Kenneth L. Beals
Oregon State University
Corvallis, Oregon

Timothy G. Baugh
University of Oklahoma
Norman, Oklahoma

Burgess Publishing Company
Minneapolis, Minnesota

0   9   8   7   6   5   4   3   2   1

Association of American Publishers, Inc.

One Park Avenue
New York, N.Y. 10016
Telephone 212 689-8920

COLLEGE DIVISION
"YOUR COMPLIMENTARY COPY AND THE PRICE OF BOOKS"

Publishers have always made complimentary copies of textbooks available because they believe a book itself is the best basis for reviewing and comparing new learning materials. They realize that professors need the opportunity to evaluate new texts with those they have been using, and to assess them as potential titles for course adoptions. The growing demand for review copies in higher education is causing concern to publishers because of the effect it will have on increasing the cost students will pay for books.

Recent statistics show, however, that review copies now account for one out of every 9 college books distributed nationally, or 11.5% of all higher education books marketed. Obviously, this represents an investment of millions and millions of dollars to the publishing industry, and has a severe impact on a publisher's costs.

In order to maintain as low a price as possible on books sold to students, the Publishers Association asks faculty to request professional review copies only if they are germane to their own discipline and course content. Professors are also urged to refrain from selling their sample, review or complimentary copies (all three terms are used interchangeably) to booksellers or individuals. Review copies disposed of in this way double the publisher's sampling costs thereby increasing the student's costs. Also, when used book dealers resell review copies they have purchased, the author is deprived of royalties on the sale of these books.

Although publishers have no desire to change the long-standing practice of giving faculty in higher education the opportunity to evaluate new instructional materials, they ask professors to request a complimentary copy only when they wish to review it for specific teaching purposes. It is expected that they will retain these books for reference or, if not, give them away to interested students.

The Association of American Publishers asks for the support of academic organizations and individual faculty members so that students, authors, professors and publishers will continue to benefit from the complimentary review practices that have been traditional in the field of higher education.

To

William E. Bittle

and

A. J. Kelso

Contents

To the Teacher

Education can be stultifying. The risk is particularly great with purely passive methods (attending lectures and reading a textbook). New approaches emphasize that learning must be done by the learner. The principle is to keep the learner actively involved, receiving feedback, and concentrating upon the important part of the subject matter.

This workbook is a hybrid text-recitation/laboratory manual. As with any compromise, specific practicality is the goal. We have three major purposes in mind:

1. To provide a more active supplement to lectures and standard textbooks.
2. To suggest a series of recitation exercises, in which the general subject matter is written, so that the instructor can devote more time to individuals.
3. To organize the material in a form more adaptable for nontraditional teaching methods, such as guided design, audio-tutorial, and personalized systems of instruction.

We hope our students—whatever their majors may be—learn to be anthropologists, rather than just be taught about anthropology. Even a standard lecture course can devote a portion of the time to practical application. This can always be done either in partial replacement of or in addition to the lecture format.

The materials required have been kept to a minimum, but the exercises are more meaningful when the students do have access to teaching aids. See the appendix for teaching notes and suggested audiovisual material.

We invite your suggestions and criticism.

To the Student

You are probably enrolled in a series of lectures which may involve several hundred other students. Such traditional lectures are efficient ways of transmitting information, since so many people can listen at the same time. Yet, there are drawbacks. It is difficult for individuals to ask questions and proceed at their own pace. Applying the knowledge is hard for a student to do alone, and the instructor is usually hard pressed to find the time for individual guidance.

Many introductory classes, therefore, devote some time to laboratories or recitations. Their goal is to enhance the lectures with some practical experience. In 1975, the Department of Anthropology at Oregon State University received funds from the State of Oregon Educational Coordinating Commission for the purpose of improving the quality of recitation sections. This workbook, along with related presentations and course of study, is the result.

Our purpose is to supplement introductory anthropology with a variety of teaching aids. These include films, videotapes, computer practice, and workbook exercises. The approach is informal and semiprogrammed. The style is conversational and deliberately meant to simulate a personal discussion with a teacher.

The workbook is focused on exercises instead of general discussion. At the same time, however, we include basic summaries which have two purposes: to provide more perspective to the exercises and to give a review of basic principles. The summaries provide the kind of information ordinarily given by an instructor. By having it written down for you, we hope to free more of the instructor's time for personal assistance.

In the ideal learning experience, you would each have a mentor expecting you to cope with and produce solutions to problems. Until you have begun to use what you have learned, it is useless and irrelevant. The purpose of science is not to memorize what has already been discovered, but to apply the knowledge and make a new contribution.

These exercises are intended to promote the process. They need not necessarily be graded, but you should at least check with the instructor to ensure that you understand. Often, it may be pleasant to work them collectively.

Most of the units are intended to be self-taught; that is, you can do them without coming to class. It is nonetheless far better to take advantage of group meetings. Moreover, some of the units require class materials. Each of them should be read prior to attending class.

Acknowledgements

We would like to thank the following people for their contributions: Thomy Smith for illustrations, Maria Beals and Carol Breazeal Vernon for editing, Dick Ross, Dr. Robert E. Bell, and Don G. Wyckoff for reading the manuscript, and Andrea Campbell and Lynne Saporito for preparing and typing the manuscript. We are further indebted to our reviewers for their suggestions, corrections, and criticism. The State of Oregon Educational Coordinating Commission made this work possible by providing funds. Despite the efforts of those cited, mistakes may remain; they are the responsibility of the authors.

Introduction

In the words of Aristotle, man is a political animal, implying that people are biological organisms joined together by social heritage and organization. This is the subject matter of anthropology.

The divisions of the science reflect the distinction between human biology and culture. The latter concept refers to the totality of learned behavior, the way we adapt to our world socially. In popular conversation, *culture* is often used to indicate snobbish refinement, such as preferring opera to bluegrass. Be aware that the anthropological definition is holistic, including virtually everything that humans make, say, and do and every way in which they live.

The critical factor is that culture must be learned from other people. The normal process of human learning is the transmission of symbols. These have meanings which are independent of any physical property. Words are prime examples of this situation. The English word *dog* has no physical resemblance to the creature in question. You could not identify the referent if you did not know the meaning which English speakers attribute to the word. The relationship is arbitrary, as it is for all symbols. A Spanish or Navaho speaker, for instance, would call the same animal by a different name.

Leslie White has given the most widely quoted illustration of symboling. Consider holy water. It has been blessed by a priest and thus endowed with a significance beyond any properties due to its particular combination of hydrogen and oxygen. No physical or chemical test could ever help you to identify holy water; the distinction lies in the sacred quality with which it is endowed.

The process of acquiring culture begins at birth. By gradually learning the meanings of the symbols a society shares, an individual member begins to know the ways of the group. Education is a form of this which emphasizes how to manipulate the symbols under a more formalized guidance.

Culture itself has a history, and the history involves the process of evolution. Understanding culture, therefore, requires the study of our remote ancestors. This is paleoanthropology—the science of human evolution.

American anthropologists traditionally divide their field into two specialties which mirror social and biological adaptations: cultural and physical anthropology.

Within the first, there are three major subfields: archaeology, social anthropology, and linguistics.

Everyone knows about archaeologists. They are the people with all their gray matter under their fingernails. They invariably have a beautiful daughter, who is continually being captured by hordes of swarming savages while her father is reading hieroglyphs in order to find the lost treasure of the forbidden city of Ouahuagadu.

Social anthropologists are the ordinary, run-of-the-mill variety. Often found on the pages of *Redbook* and *Cosmopolitan,* their articles relate their experiences of living among the Hehe or the Susu and offer their advice on breast feeding.

Linguistic anthropologists have a less well defined public image, since nobody knows about them. Due to their well-deserved obscurity, they are often presumed to be prescriptive grammarians who are waiting to snub you for saying *ain't* or splitting infinitives.

Physical anthropologists are a bunch of creeps. Much of their time is spent giving long, enigmatic names to fossils. They have a bizarre affection for measuring people's heads so that they can find out what race they belong to. They like to travel all over the world to collect ear wax, blood, and spit.

Such stereotypes aside, anthropologists as a group want to know why people vary. They are interested in how the variation relates to our biological history, our social tradition, and the total ecology of the environment. The questions are those of basic human curiosity. Where did we come from? What were our ancestors like? How do the lives of other people compare to our own? How and why do people act, look, and speak differently? Anthropology will not give you a clear and simple answer to any of these questions, but it should at least broaden your thinking about humanity everywhere and the long process of evolution.

Since anthropology deliberately adopts such a broad perspective, populations all over the world are visited. The social anthropologist has the task of describing their cultural practices. The best way to do this is from firsthand observation instead of reading, hearing, or guessing about it. In some cases, several years of field work are needed. Participation in a population's daily activities often supplies more insight than would merely asking questions.

The observations resulting from such a study are recorded in an ethnography. This is a report informing other scientists about the culture of the particular population. Finally, social anthropologists compare societies so that they can test theories about why people behave as they do.

Linguistic anthropology is a specialization within cultural anthropology which concentrates upon language. Linguists have developed methods for making a written record of any language spoken by any ethnic group. Their major purpose is not to learn how to speak languages but to analyze their structures. They are concerned with questions about how languages originated, how they are related, and how various ways of speaking influence various ways of thinking and acting.

Archaeologists do dig for things, but this is only a part of their work. Actually, more time is spent in the laboratory, where the evidence of human life in the past is examined and evaluated. An archaeologist seeks information—not artifacts or treasure. The objects themselves have scientific value only in regard to their context.

Physical anthropology is also divided into specialties. Human paleontology focuses upon our evolutionary record. Heterography (sometimes called human population biology) examines biological variation among contemporary groups. Some physical anthropologists recognize a third field, cultural biology, which is the study of the relationship between biology and culture. It seeks to integrate the several specializations.

Most introductory courses begin with paleoanthropology, which refers to human life in the past and combines both physical anthropology and archaeology. From this beginning, you should gain a broader perspective into both cultural and biological evolution.

Integration of the different parts of an introductory course is important. Otherwise, what you are studying is an unrelated hodgepodge. The workbook is mostly summary review and exercises. You will gain more from it by always trying to see the relevance of the information to the total natural history of our species. One way to do this is by constantly reminding yourself that human variation in the past and present is always determined by the interaction of the natural environment, biological heritage, and the record of cultural adaptations.

CHAPTER 1
The Primates

There are two sources of biological and cultural information concerning modern humans: the paleontological and archaeological record and examination of other living animals. Humans belong to the order Primates, and all of us share part of a common evolutionary heritage. Taking cognizance of man as a primate gives us a broader perspective on ourselves. This unit summarizes some basic information about primates and includes an exercise on primate locomotion.

CLASSIFICATION

There are 189 living species of primates. As with all organisms, they are grouped according to the degree of evolutionary relationship they share. Knowledge of the taxonomic names is essential to following a description of the various classifications.

The order Primates has three suborders: the prosimians, platyrrhines, and catarrhines. Prosimians are the most primitive and form the ancestral group from which platyrrhines and catarrhines evolved. Most have long snouts. Except for the tarsier, they have a moist area of skin at the end of the nose (a rhinarium). Their eye sockets (orbits) are confluent with depressions on either side of the head (temporal fossae). The groups, examples, and distributions are shown in table 1.1.

TABLE 1.1
Suborder Prosimii

SUPERFAMILY	FAMILY	EXAMPLES	DISTRIBUTION
Tupaioidea	Tupaiidae	Tree shrews	Southeast Asia
Lemuroidea	Lemuridae	Lemurs	Madagascar
	Indridae	Indri, sifaka	Madagascar
	Daubentoniidae	Aye-aye	Madagascar
Lorisoidea	Lorisidae	Loris, potto	South Asia, West Africa
	Galagidae	Bushbaby	Africa
Tarsioidea	Tarsiidae	Tarsier	Indonesia, Philippines

TABLE 1.2
Suborder Platyrrhinae

SUPERFAMILY	FAMILY	EXAMPLES	DISTRIBUTION
Ceboidea	Callithricidae	Marmosets, tamarins	Panama to southern Brazil
	Cebidae	Sakis, titis, howler monkey, squirrel monkey	Southern Mexico to Argentina

TABLE 1.3
Superfamily Cercopithecoidea

FAMILY	SUBFAMILY	EXAMPLES	DISTRIBUTION
Cercopithecidae	Colobinae	Langurs, gueraza, proboscis monkey	India, Indochina, Tibet, Sumatra, Borneo, Ethiopia
	Cercopithecinae	Macaques, mangabeys, guenons, baboons, drills, mandrills	Africa through Arabia, India, and Japan

There is a trend today toward not including the tree shrews (Tupaioidea) as primates. Morphologically, tree shrews are intermediate between primates and insectivores, such as moles and true shrews. Phylogenetically, the tree shrews have had a long period of independent evolution, but they have apparently changed very little for the last 80 million years.

Platyrrhines are primates found only in the New World: North, Central, and South America. Some platyrrhines have grasping, or prehensile, tails. All of them have 3 premolar teeth on both sides of the jaw on both the upper and lower jaws. There is thus a total of 12 premolars. The cartilage between the nostrils is broad, and the nostrils themselves point toward the side of the face. There is but one superfamily, which has two families.

The suborder Catarrhinae contains the Old World monkeys, apes, and humans. Catarrhines have two premolar teeth on both sides of both the upper and lower jaws, making a total of eight. Their nostrils point downward rather than toward the side. Since people are catarrhines, we shall list the taxonomy in a slightly more detailed fashion. The first group (or taxon) to consider is the Old World monkeys, all of whom belong to the superfamily Cercopithecoidea.

The remaining superfamily of the catarrhines is Hominoidea. This comprises apes and humans together. Hominoids, unlike monkeys, do not have tails. In addition to this, the first lower molars of apes and humans normally have five cusps rather than four as do monkeys. There are two groups of apes: the lesser apes, including gibbons and the siamang, and the greater apes, including the orangutan, gorilla, and chimpanzees. You should be familiar with hominoid taxonomy for all of the living genera.

It is critical to know the scientific names in table 1.4, and there is no way of doing this other than by memory. So, memorize. If your lecturer says, for instance, that *Ramapithecus* is the earliest known hominid, the statement is meaningless if you cannot follow the taxonomic implication.

TABLE 1.4
Superfamily Hominoidea

FAMILY	GENUS	EXAMPLES	NO. OF SPECIES	DISTRIBUTION
Hylobatidae	*Hylobates*	Gibbons	7	Indonesia, Southeast Asia
	Symphalangus	Siamang	1	Sumatra
Pongidae	*Pongo*	Orangutan	1	Sumatra, Borneo
	Pan	Chimpanzees	2	Africa
	Gorilla	Gorilla	1	Africa
Hominidae	*Homo*	Human	1	Global (and spatial)

A word about names. Each scientific name is binomial. Let's take an illustration. The siamang is *Symphalangus syndactylus.* The first name refers to the genus; it should begin with a capital letter. The second name refers to the particular species in the genus; it should never be capitalized. It is traditional to underline the full name to indicate italics. Do not try to make the names plural; they already are. Do not add apostrophes or make any change whatsoever. One person is *Homo sapiens;* any number of people are still *Homo sapiens.* If you wish to abbreviate a scientific name, there is only one correct way to do so. Place a period after the first letter of the genus and write the specific name in full. To illustrate:

D. madagascariensis stands for *Daubentonia madagascariensis*—the aye-aye

P. paniscus stands for *Pan paniscus*—the pygmy chimpanzee

The following sentences were written by a student. Find the mistakes and write the sentences correctly in the space provided.

"Homo Erectus is a pongoid specie. Erectus's leg bones are like a homo's Sapien."

Check the rewritten version at the end of the unit.

PRIMATE EVOLUTION

Geologists have a hierarchial classification of time. The most comprehensive division is an era. Eras, in turn, are divided into periods, and periods are often divided into epochs. It is not possible to discuss any evolutionary record without reference to time. You will therefore need to know the sequence of geological history. The eras and periods are listed in table 1.5.

During the Permian period, a group of mammallike reptiles (therapsids) first occur in the fossil record. They became common in the succeeding Triassic period. The therapsids were the ancestral stock of all mammals. About 180 million years ago, the therapsids evolved into the earliest primitive mammals. Most of these early types became extinct without leaving descendants. A few species, however, did evolve into the ancestors of the mammals at the present time. Some of the changes which were taking place were these: (1) more efficient locomotion was obtained by bringing the legs more directly underneath the body mass; (2) adaptations were occurring for more uniform regulation of body heat—the acquisition of hair is an example; and (3) a placenta was evolved which resulted in important reproductive changes—the offspring developed within the mother rather than being deposited as an egg in a nest.

All of these circumstances are found in nearly all the contemporary mammals. They were present by the time of the Cretaceous.

One group of Cretaceous mammals had a life-style and superficial appearance similar to squirrels. A major difference is that their diet consisted mainly of grubs and insects rather than nuts. This group represents the early insectivores.

An adaptive radiation among the early insectivores occurred around the Mesozoic-Cenozoic boundary. Some of the primitive insectivores began to specialize in gliding. Their descendants became the bats. Another group did not change as much but did move toward a more terrestrial way of life. Their descendants are the living insectivores, such as shrews and moles. Yet a third group became more specialized for arboreal life by gradually developing grasping hands and feet. This group did not climb by sticking their claws into the bark for support. Instead, the support was obtained by wrapping an entire appendage around branches; this action is the most fundamental mark of a primate. Given this grasping form of locomotion, claws became a detriment. They were slowly replaced by weaker and flatter nails. Human hands are a constant reminder of our arboreal heritage. Our feet, however, are quite atypical and have been greatly modified for bipedal walking instead of grasping.

TABLE 1.5
Some Major Events of Geological History

ERA	PERIOD	AGE (IN MILLIONS OF YEARS)	EVENTS
Cenozoic	Quaternary	2	Evolution of modern humans
	Tertiary	65	Divergence and evolution of primates
Mesozoic	Cretaceous	150	Divergence of insectivores, early modern mammals
	Jurassic	180	Primitive mammals
	Triassic	200	Thecodont and therapsid reptiles
Paleozoic	Permian	225	Early reptiles common, cotylosaurs, mammallike reptiles, therapsids
	Carboniferous	300	Coal deposits formed
	Devonian	330	Land plants abundant, primitive amphibians, labyrinthodonts, crossopterygians
	Silurian	400	First jawed chordates (placoderms), some land plants
	Ordovician	500	First chordates (ostracoderms
	Cambrian	600	Invertebrates only
	Precambrian		

Primate evolution takes place in the Cenozoic. You will need to memorize the names of Cenozoic periods and epochs in their proper order. This information is given in table 1.6. Study it.

Some geologists prefer to separate the Quaternary into two epochs rather than one as given. Under this system, the Pleistocene was followed by the Holocene about 10,000 years ago. Other geologists argue that we are still in the Pleistocene. The main objective is to remember the sequence. It will help you if you observe that the first letters of the Tertiary epochs form the mnemonic word PEOMP.

Primates are first found in North America, in the region around the northern Rocky Mountains. Tropical climates existed at that time all the way to the Canadian border. Primates also began to be found in Europe during the later part of the Paleocene. They did not have to swim the Atlantic Ocean to get there; North America, Greenland, and Europe were still partially connected landmasses. Recently, a new primate genus, *Azebius*, from Africa has also been discovered in Paleocene deposits.

There is some uncertainty about the earliest genus. One questionable candidate is *Purgatorius* from the very early Paleocene. Other paleontologists believe *Purgatorius* is an insectivore and not a primate. There was not much difference between ancient primates and insectivores, so it is difficult to distinguish between them. As time passed, the differences gradually became more pronounced.

Excluding the questionable case of *Purgatorius*, the genus *Plesiadapis* is the earliest known. This fossil material dates from the middle and late Paleocene. Different *Plesiadapis* species ranged from

TABLE 1.6
Major Events of Primate Evolution in the Cenozoic Era

PERIOD	EPOCH	AGE (IN MILLIONS OF YEARS)	EVENTS
Quaternary	Pleistocene	2	Appearance of *Homo,* our own genus
Tertiary	Pliocene	6	Earliest hominids (*Ramapithecus* and later *Australopithecus*)
	Miocene	23	Adaptive radiation of apes, last common ancestor of apes and hominids
	Oligocene	36	Beginning of first catarrhines, Old World monkeys, and apes; decline of prosimians in number and variety
	Eocene	58	Florescence and diversification of prosimians
	Paleocene	65	Origin of Primates (primitive prosimians)

the size of a rat to that of a cat. All of them had peculiar rodentlike incisors, and long claws were present on the digits instead of nails. Superficially, *Plesiadapis* resembled a possum with ratlike front teeth and lemurlike back teeth. The genus is now believed to have become extinct during the Eocene. The rodentlike incisors of *Plesiadapis* are specialized, and some authorities take this as evidence that they were not in the direct lineage of any living primate. Others believe the family may be ancestral to tarsiers. At any rate, *Plesiadapis* serves as a good example of the general stage of primate evolution during the Paleocene.

The Eocene marks a time of prosimian diversification. Prosimians became more modern in appearance, and there were a great number and a great variety of them. As yet, they remained the only kinds of primates in the fossil record. Toward the end of the Eocene, some of the prosimians had acquired some of the characteristics of the catarrhines. One genus in particular (*Amphipithecus*) is thought to be in the direct line of catarrhine evolution. It may have been the last common ancestor of apes and Old World monkeys, which began to differentiate during the following Oligocene.

During the Oligocene, there was a widespread florescence of most groups of mammals. Since then, the number and variety of mammals have been gradually declining. The prosimians themselves began to decline, probably due to competition with rodents and early monkeys. The roots of monkeys, lesser apes, and greater apes can all be traced to an Oligocene origin. Two genera are especially significant in regard to human evolution: *Aegyptopithecus* and *Propliopithecus.* The former is almost certainly a common ancestor of pongids and hominids. The latter is more slightly built and similar to a gibbon but more generalized. Some authorities believe *Propliopithecus* was a primitive gibbon; others think it may be the ancestor of *Aegyptopithecus.*

It is convenient to consider Miocene and Pliocene catarrhines together since some lived during portions of both epochs. We will only mention hominoids. (Remember that this refers to both apes and humans.) At one time, more than two dozen genera of hominoids were believed to have existed during the Miocene or Pliocene. Today there are only five which are usually recognized.

Let's explain this circumstance since it also bears upon the interpretation of human phylogeny. When paleontologists believe they have discovered a new genus or species (and provide evidence in a standard manner), they are entitled to give the discovery a name. Often this must be done with fragmentary evidence, since it is a great rarity to discover an ancient but complete primate skeleton. Suppose a discovery was made, and a new name was bestowed: *Alphonsopithecus ridiculous.* Suppose that later someone reexamined the material and demonstrated that the remains actually belonged to a taxon which had already been described. This means that *Alphonsopithecus ridiculous* never existed. The fossil specimens attributed to it must go to the name which was given first. Circumstances similar to this are quite common, and they can create a great deal of understandable confusion.

The process of reassignment has reduced the number of known Miocene-Pliocene hominoid genera to five. However, at one time or another (or by one specialist or another) all five have been claimed to be either in or very near the direct line of human evolution. These five are: *Dryopithecus, Oreopithecus, Gigantopithecus, Ramapithecus,* and *Australopithecus.*

Gigantopithecus is a large ape, probably about twice the size of the modern gorilla. One species from China, *G. blacki,* occurs far too late in time to be a human ancestor. It dates from the late Pliocene and extends well into the Pleistocene. This makes the species contemporary with early humans. Some rather far-out speculations romantically suggest that descendants of *Gigantopithecus* are still around in the form of the Sasquatch and Yeti—we leave this to your imagination.

The second species, *G. bilasperensis,* is much older. It has been found in late Miocene deposits in India which were formed about 9 million years ago. It is presumed to be the ancestor of later Chinese forms. However, *Gigantopithecus* is unlikely to be in the direct line of hominid descent. The major reason for this conclusion is that other hominoid genera occur even earlier and show a greater similarity to later hominids.

The phylogenetic interpretation of *Oreopithecus,* a genus dating from the middle and late Miocene, has long been disputed. One argument against a direct relationship to hominids is based on the presence of an extra cusp on the teeth. This cusp is not found in any other primate from the Oligocene except *Apidium.* Most specialists see the genus as a descendant of *Apidium* and representing a line of evolution parallel to that of the pongids.

Omitting *Gigantopithecus* and *Oreopithecus* from our direct ancestry still leaves three remaining genera to consider. *Australopithecus* is universally recognized as a hominid, indicating that the divergence between pongids and hominids must have started at some earlier time, probably in the middle Miocene around 14 million years ago.

Dryopithecus lived during this time and is typically regarded as the last common ancestor of hominids and great apes. Several species have been reported in Europe, Africa, and Asia. Some of them are regarded as ancestral to particular living apes: *D. indicus* to the orangutan, *D. major* to the gorilla, and *D. africanus* to the chimp. Controversy and uncertainty surround hypotheses in regard to the origin of hominids from *Dryopithecus.* One presumed descendant, *Ramapithecus,* is widely regarded as the earliest hominid. However, only teeth, palate, and jaw fragments of the genus have been discovered so far. The canine teeth differ from the large canines of living apes; in *Ramapithecus,* they protrude only slightly. The hominid status of the material is nonetheless not uniformly accepted. One alternative view is that *Ramapithecus* is another Miocene ape and a member of the widespread dryopithecines.

There is no ultimate truth in paleontology. Each interpretation of the fossil record is an inference, based upon limited information and reflecting different philosophical attitudes about narrow and broad classification. In the summary pages which follow, the emphasis is heuristic: intended for a specific learning goal rather than statement of intellectual finality. Important genera are listed beside an unqualified comment reflecting the simplest interpretation of their evolutionary significance. The testing of such hypotheses occupies much of the attention of specialists involved in the frustrating and fascinating search for our origin.

TABLE 1.7
Fossil Primates and Their Evolutionary Significance

EPOCH	GENUS	HYPOTHESIS[1]
Miocene-Pliocene	*Australopithecus*	Ancestor of *Homo erectus* _____ _____
	Ramapithecus	Earliest known hominid_____ _____
	Gigantopithecus	Largest ape, not directly related to hominids_____ _ _____
	Oreopithecus	Widely disputed genus, shows parallel evolution with pongids and hominids _____ _____
	Dryopithecus	Widespread genus of apes, last common ancestor of hominids and pongids _____ _____
Oligocene	*Aegyptopithecus*	Earliest great ape, ancestor of *Dryopithecus* _____ _____
	Propliopithecus	Generalized ape morphology, ancestral to *Aegyptopithecus* (others see it as more gibbonlike) _____ _____
	Aeolopithecus *Pliopithecus*	Early gibbonlike apes, not as specialized for brachiation _____
	Apidium	Ancestor of *Oreopithecus,* same family as *Parapithecus* _____
	Parapithecus	First Old World monkey _____ _____

[1] Space is provided for you to add notes, qualifications, or comments.

TABLE 1.7 (continued)

EPOCH	GENUS	HYPOTHESIS
Eocene	*Amphipithecus*	Ancestor of catarrhines _____
	Necrolemur	Ancestor of tarsier _____
	Adapis *Protoadapis*	European prosimians ancestral to lemurs_____
	Notharctus	North American prosimian demonstrating evolutionary advance compared to Paleocene _____
Paleocene	*Plesiadapis*	Very primitive North American prosimian with specialized teeth, earliest undisputed primate _____
	Purgatorius	Intermediate genus with both insectivore and primate traits _____

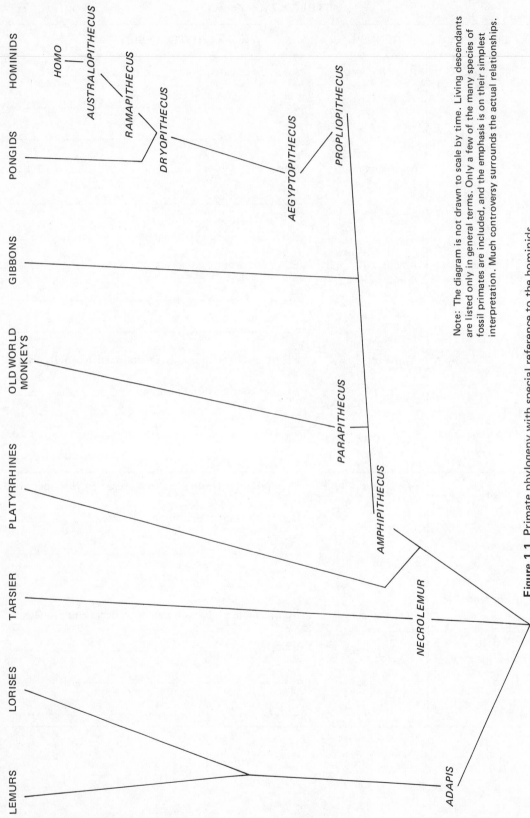

Figure 1.1. Primate phylogeny with special reference to the hominids.

Note: The diagram is not drawn to scale by time. Living descendants are listed only in general terms. Only a few of the many species of fossil primates are included, and the emphasis is on their simplest interpretation. Much controversy surrounds the actual relationships.

EXERCISE: PRIMATE LOCOMOTION

In recent years, anthropologists have become particularly interested in primate locomotion. There are several reasons for this. One of them is that morphology and behavior are closely connected. Another is that the investigation of how living primates locomote provides insight into an interpretation of the anatomy of fossil forms. Finally, there is a considerable amount of debate about the sequence of evolutionary events which eventually led to the unique bipedal walking of human beings.

We want you to discover how the proportions of body parts can be related to ways of moving and acting. In a subsequent class period, you should see some demonstrations of the actual ways in which primates move. Predictions can be made by measuring the relative lengths of body parts.

There are five patterns. Practice them yourself, and see if you can determine the most efficient ratios of arm and leg length.

Vertical Clinging and Leaping

The trunk is held vertical. Support is gained by grasping with both hands and feet. To move, the hands are taken from the branch, and the leg muscles are used to push the body forward. The galago and tarsier are especially adapted for this locomotor pattern.

Quadrupedalism

Try walking on all fours with the palms and soles (not the knees) on the ground. Notice how much easier this is if the knees are used instead. Why? Are your long legs disadvantageous? Notice your gait. Did you move your legs in a diagonal sequence? Why? Virtually none of the nonprimate quadrupeds use such a diagonal gait. Baboons and tree shrews are examples of quadrupedal primates.

Knuckle-walking

This is practiced by the gorilla and chimpanzee. It is the same as quadrupedalism except that the front weight is borne by the knuckles instead of the palms or digits. Note that the trunk is partially erect and that the body is inclined at about a 45° angle instead of being horizontal or vertical.

Brachiation

Do not try this without a very strong support such as a rope or bar. The hands grasp a branch. All the body weight is suspended below. The legs dangle in space. One hand is removed. The shoulders are rotated, and the free hand reaches forward to grasp again. The arm-swinging, hand-over-hand pattern is repeated to move forward. A few New World monkeys are adapted for brachiation. The gibbon is extremely adept at it.

Bipedalism

Humans are the only habitually bipedal primates. Occasionally, other primates will walk on their hind limbs, but this is not their normal means of progression. Some nonprimates (such as birds and kangaroos) are also bipeds, but their walking gait is very different from that of humans. When people walk, the heel strikes first. The weight is shifted to the big toe while the remaining leg is brought forward. A remarkable balancing, weight-shifting action by our muscles prevents us from falling. Walking is the most basic distinction between the human species and the other primates. In adapting us to it, evolution changed the shape of our feet, legs, pelvis, and spinal cord.

If you did experiment with some of these types of locomotion, you certainly recognize that relative arm and leg length has a lot to do with it. There is a ratio which expresses both proportions together. This is the intermembral index.

$$\text{Intermembral index} = \frac{\text{humerus length} + \text{radius length}}{\text{femur length} + \text{tibia length}} \times 100$$

The humerus and radius are two of the bones in the forelimb (arms in people). The femur and tibia are two of the bones in the hindlimb (our legs). To calculate the intermembral index, you need to recognize the four bones involved. They are marked on the accompanying skeletal diagrams of selected primates.

Measure the maximum length of all four bones. A ruler's accuracy is satisfactory. Insert the measurements into the formula on the preceding page. You multiply by 100 to remove the decimal place. Determine the intermembral index for each of the specimens. It varies in living primates from about 50 to 150. A ratio of 100 means that the arms and legs are the same length. A ratio of 150 means that the legs are only two-thirds as long as the arms.

The intermembral index correlates with the type of locomotion to which a primate is adapted. Based upon your experiments with different kinds of movement, you should be able to predict the locomotor type of each specimen you measure. *Notharctus,* for example, is an Eocene prosimian which (obviously) no one has seen in movement. Its intermembral index is 60. What type of locomotion do you think it used? What types are the following three mystery primates? Refer to the exercise supplement at the end of the chapter when you have finished for further explanation.

Mystery Primate A

Intermembral index _____

Predicted locomotor type _____

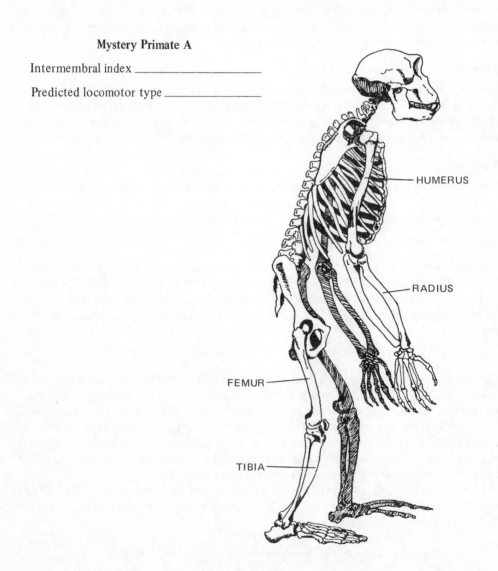

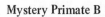

Mystery Primate B

Intermembral index _____

Predicted locomotor type _____

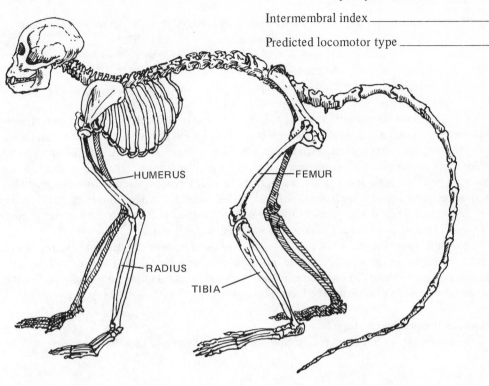

HUMERUS

FEMUR

RADIUS

TIBIA

Mystery Primate C

Intermembral index _____

Predicted locomotor type _____

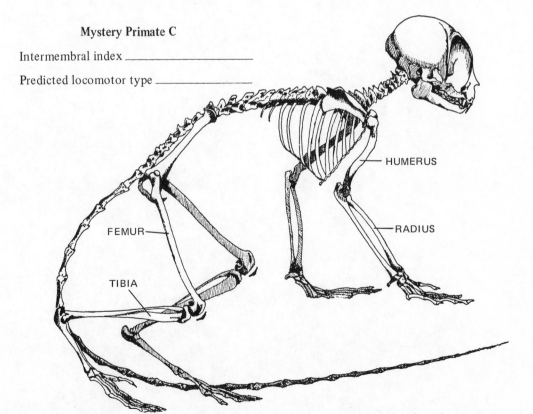

HUMERUS

RADIUS

FEMUR

TIBIA

EXERCISE SUPPLEMENT

The general ranges of intermembral index among types of primate locomotion are these:

Vertical clingers and leapers	50 to 65
Quadrupeds	75 to 100
Brachiators	108 to 150
Knuckle-walkers	110 to 120
Bipeds (humans)	70

You should use some caution when applying the table to the skeletal measurements. Evolutionary theory proposes that anatomical adaptation over a long period of time accommodates an animal group to a behavior that it practices. This is a long-term process. An animal that has altered its behavior in the recent past may not have a theoretically ideal anatomical structure to support that behavior. In addition, arms and legs have uses other than for locomotion, and evolution must be a compromise between different pressures. For example, baboons have longer arms than would be expected for quadrupeds. While this may reflect their ancestry, it probably relates to the fact that their arms are used in feeding and reaching for fruits as well as in locomotion.

A second reason for caution is that primates may use a number of different patterns of movement for different purposes. For instance, macaque monkeys, though they are normally quadrupeds, sometimes traverse short distances on two legs. The intermembral index is thus only part of the information needed to reconstruct the locomotor pattern.

Answer to the problem on page 6:

Homo erectus is a hominid species. *Homo erectus* leg bones are like *Homo sapiens*.

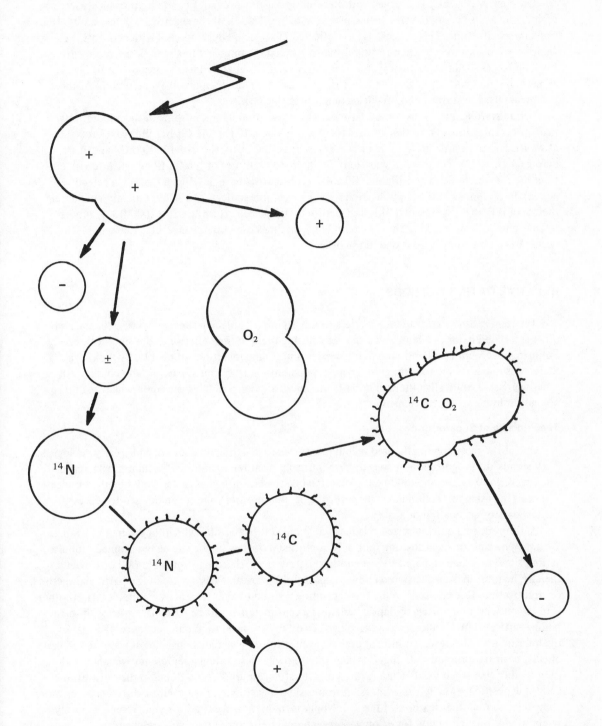

CHAPTER 2
Dating Methods

Our society is greatly concerned with the concept of time. Most of us live by the clock. Getting up in the morning, going to class, eating meals, watching TV—all of these activities demand our attention at a specific time. This concern is also reflected in science. Physicists deal with concepts such as velocity, which is a measurement of the distance covered by an object in a specific amount of time. In reconstructing human prehistory, anthropologists must deal with linear time in order to place archaeological or paleontological sites in a given sequence. This chapter will examine some of the techniques used by anthropologists in accomplishing this task.

Before starting our discussion of dating methods, we should look at some of the annotations made concerning time. Our calendar uses the designations B.C. (before Christ) and A.D. (*Anno Domini*). The correct usage of these markers is to place B.C. after the date (5000 B.C.) and A.D. before (A.D. 1975). But these designations are limited to cultures of the Christian faith. Jewish cultures use a different form and Islamic still another. Scientists have developed their own calendrical system. In textbooks or other publications dealing with this subject, you will frequently encounter the use of B.P. (before present). This designation is also placed after the date (2000 B.P.), and its reference point is A.D. 1950. These systems are sometimes used interchangeably. You will be expected to be able to shift from one to the other.

RELATIVE DATING METHODS

The term *relative dating methods* refers to the problem of placing sites, remains, artifacts, and other associated items in a temporal sequence (placing them in time relative to one another). For example, if we went to a family reunion we might find four generations of people. By looking at them, we should be able to distinguish great-grandparents, grandparents, parents, and children. In other words, we could align them in order from oldest to youngest. This is exactly what the anthropologist is doing with his specimens.

The Principle of Superposition

One of the most commonly used techniques for relative dating was developed by early geologists. They surmised the deposition of soils to have normally occurred in an orderly and uniform action. The first or lowest deposit would be the oldest, while the last or highest layer would be the youngest. The basis for using this technique is the principle of superposition, and it can be used to represent the raw data of occupation of a site.

Anthropologists quickly seized this idea and applied it to the sites which they were excavating. With the principle of superposition, not only could the sequence in one site be determined, but also various sites could be compared to one another. Before the archaeologist puts a shovel or trowel into the dirt, he must make a decision on how to control the vertical levels by selecting a particular method of stratification. One choice is to use the depositional strata of soils to achieve natural levels. Another is to establish arbitrary levels of depth; perhaps 10 centimeters might be used. The process of maintaining vertical controls allows an archaeologist to establish the stratigraphic sequence. Because of the human factor, however, additional problems are involved when an archaeologist uses the principle of superposition for relative dating. Consider the following case as being representative. Many cultures tend to bury their dead or use earthen pits for storage purposes. By doing so they disturb the beds of deposition. Usually these intrusions can easily be accounted for by subtle differences in color, compactness, and other features of the soil. Nonhuman disturbances may also be present, but only rarely would rodent activity, for example, present any confusion to the expert analyst.

Examine figures 2.1 and 2.2 and verify the relative age of the artifact series. The most basic rules of interpretation are these:

1. In undisturbed strata, the oldest is at the bottom.
2. Anything in an intrusion is younger than anything intruded upon.
3. In the same stratum, deeper objects are normally older than shallower objects.

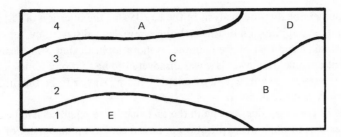

Figure 2.1. Undisturbed stratigraphy with four layers (1, 2, 3, and 4). The artifacts found in the site are represented by letters. There are no intrusions, and the stratigraphic sequence is E—B—C—D—A.

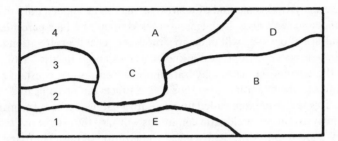

Figure 2.2. A site with an intrusion. Stratum 4 intrudes through 3 and into 2. Anything in stratum 4 is younger than anything the stratum intrudes upon. The sequence of artifacts is E—B—D—C—A.

Fluorine Dating

A second method of relative dating involves the quantitative chemical analysis of bone. In this respect, the method of fluorine dating is somewhat limited for it cannot be used on any other material. But if we have human skeletal remains found in association with extinct animal bones, we are able to determine if they are of the same age. Fluorine dating depends upon phosphate replacement in the bone by fluorine found in groundwater. In a single location, this replacement occurs at a fairly constant rate. This allows for comparison in a particular site. However, such a method cannot be applied in comparing two sites. Groundwater in different locations may contain different chemical percentages. And, if there is more fluorine in one area than another, phosphate replacement will occur at a more rapid rate. This problem is further complicated by our incomplete understanding of the absorption of chemical elements by bone. We do know that climatic conditions will also affect the absorption rate. Hence, caution must be used in this (as in any other) procedure.

Probably the most dramatic use of fluorine analysis occurred when the Piltdown remains were revealed to be a hoax. The story began early in the twentieth century when a man by the name of Charles Dawson discovered a modern-looking skull and an apelike mandible, or lower jaw. The stratigraphy of the site was evaluated, and the age of the remains were calculated on this basis. Dawson turned his finds over to Sir Arthur Keith, who was one of the foremost paleontologists of the day. Keith examined and reconstructed the Piltdown material. He cane to the conclusion that the human brain had evolved earlier than other parts of the head. This position was not a popular one outside of England, where the Piltdown specimens were found. Scholars on the continent decided to test Keith's ability. First they measured the cranial capacity of a human skull. Then the cranium was smashed and given to Keith to reconstruct. With patience and skill, Keith worked with the fragments until he had them in the proper order. Another calculation of the cranial capacity was made, and much to the astonishment of the European scholars, it was extremely close to the original measurement. As an additional test of the Piltdown remains, an X ray was taken. Still nothing was found to be out of the ordinary. Thus, these remains were accepted as enigmatic but authentic fossils.

With the development of fluorine analysis in the late 1940s, the question of Piltdown once again came to the forefront. The application of this technique revealed a discrepancy between the content of fluorine in the mandible and that of the cranium. A more sophisticated X-ray scan was made, and to the embarrassment of some, the lower jaw was discovered to be that of a female orangutan. Piltdown then became recognized as a fraud. Many people believe Dawson to be the originator of the hoax, but the true story is still unknown.

The significance of this story does not lie in the fact that these scientists had been outwitted, but rather in the idea that through the application of new techniques, the pursuit of knowledge can be advanced even if only by small increments.

Obsidian Hydration

A more recent development in the area of relative dating is the technique known as obsidian hydration. Like fluorine analysis, this method of relative dating can be applied only to a specific kind of material. Obsidian, or volcanic glass, is an igneous rock containing a high percentage of aluminum. A freshly exposed surface of obsidian will undergo a process of chemical alteration triggered by a reaction with atmospheric water. This process is known as hydration. Relative dating using this method is based on the assumption that the hydration process occurs at a constant rate. Thus, by measuring the thickness of the hydration layer, obsidian artifacts can be compared to their relative time of production. This technique is included under relative dating methods for many of the same reasons as fluorine analysis. Different climatic conditions will vary the rate of hydration, which is in itself still improperly understood. Also, the chemical composition of obsidian found in one part of the world may differ from that found in another, and such differences may have an effect on the rate of hydration.

By these and other means, we have seen how physical anthropologists and archaeologists may be able to establish a sequence of events at a site. The knowledge obtained from individual sites may be compared to give a more complete picture of human development.

CHRONOMETRIC DATING METHODS

Chronometric dating methods are ones that can be tied into a calendrical system. This means that the phenomena measured can be placed directly in time. To return to the example of the family reunion, we could ask the same people to give their birthdates instead of basing our conclusions on appearance. Then we would be able to align these individuals precisely on a continuum based upon their calendrical age. This is the primary goal of chronometric dating techniques.

Dendrochronology

One of the first absolute dating methods to be applied by anthropologists was tree-ring dating, or dendrochronology. About 1913, an astronomer (Andrew E. Douglas) was attempting to correlate the appearance of sunspots with climatic conditions as revealed by tree rings in the American Southwest. Scientists have known for many years that a tree acquires an annual growth ring during the spring and summer months. By simply counting the number of circles, the age of any tree can be determined accurately. The problem is how to extend these counts far enough in time for them to be useful. Noticing the effects of average annual rainfall on the size of the increments provided the solution. During wet years, tree rings tend to be thick, while dry years produce thin rings. By studying these rings, scientists can create a master chart for a specific type of tree. Conifers, such as the Ponderosa pine (*Pinus ponderosa*) or bristlecone pine (*Pinus aristata*), are the most useful. The master chart is started with a core sample from an older living tree. It may provide a fifty-year segment into the past. The next step might involve finding the same species of tree in an abandoned ranch house. Here, another core sample is taken. In order to relate the second specimen to the first, a certain amount of overlap between the two is necessary. If they do overlap, our chart may now be nearly ninety years in length. This same process is continued through the finding of older and older buildings until the chart may be extended into the past by several thousands of years. An archaeologist who encounters a house site in which the crossbeams are of the same species as the master chart can simply take a core sample and compare the annual growth patterns to the chart until he finds the corresponding section. This gives him some idea of when the tree was cut. Remember though, the sample may not provide an accurate date for the house itself, since the beam may have been removed from an earlier house or building. But dendrochronology does identify the earliest possible date of construction.

Dendrochronology has been used most extensively in arid regions where there is a wide fluctuation in the average annual rainfall. This ensures an irregular growth pattern from year to year. One should also be careful to use trees from an area in which there is only one controlling factor in the size of the tree rings. If the thickness of the increments is uniform, then the tree is almost useless for this type of dating. Thus, care must be taken not to use trees that have tapped a permanent source of groundwater, such as those near a river bed. Dendrochronology is at the present time the most accurate dating method devised. Unfortunately, its application is limited; it can be used only in areas of the world meeting certain stringent conditions.

Radiocarbon Dating

Radiocarbon dating, on the other hand, is not limited spatially. Cosmic radiation constantly bombards our atmosphere and produces neutrons that react with an isotope of nitrogen (^{14}N). Such reactions result in a radioactive form of carbon (^{14}C). Carbon 14 is unstable and attempts to return to the more consistent form of nitrogen by emitting beta particles. Conversion from ^{14}C to nitrogen occurs at a constant rate, with one-half of the total radioactive carbon being transformed about every 5700 years. This information alone tells us very little, but coupled with the knowledge that ^{14}C reacts with oxygen in the same way as the stable form of carbon (^{12}C), it provides us with an important key. All living creatures from snapdragons to human beings absorb a certain amount of carbon (including ^{14}C) from the atmosphere until their death. By establishing the presence of radioactive carbon to have been more or less constant from the present throughout the range of prehistory, scientists were then able to measure the percentage of ^{14}C and determine the age of the specimen. This is accomplished by assuming the organic material to have had a complete complement of radioactive carbon prior to the death of its constituent parts. Since the exchange with the atmosphere is discontinued at this point, the ^{14}C can be converted to carbon dioxide gas, and the number of beta radiations can then be determined by a sophisticated Geiger counter. If the beta radiations are one-half of those of a living organism, we know the specimen is about 5700 years old. If they radiate one-fourth this amount, the age is approximately 11,400 years.

The term *estimate* is important in understanding the process. There is always the possibility that the sample has been contaminated by the presence of modern carbon. This can occur by soil acids, plant roots, or techniques used for preservation. Factors such as these can create a certain amount of error. The accuracy of the technique has been checked against the results obtained by dendrochronology. By this means, it was determined that radiocarbon dates start to diverge from true calendar dates after about 1500 B.C. (3450 B.P.). This introduces another source of error in an evaluation of the sample if it is of greater antiquity. Only in recent publications have the dates been corrected for the radiocarbon-dendrochronology divergence.

Yet another source of error is the fact that figuring radioactive disintegration involves a statistical approach. The number of emissions varies slightly even in samples of the same age. This variation is measured by standard deviation, which is a statistical measurement of the amount of variability in a set of data. There is a 68% probability that the true measurement will fall within one standard deviation of the mean. Within two standard deviations, the probability is 95%. Three raise the probability to 99.74%.

A radiocarbon date is followed by its standard deviation, indicated with a plus or minus sign. For instance, a date might be 11,400 B.P.±500. This means that 68% of the time, the true date will fall between 10,900 and 11,900 B.P. If we double the standard deviation (to 1000 in this case), we know there is a 95% probability that the date lies between 10,400 and 12,400 B.P. As you see, the greater the probability of the limits of the date, the broader the time interval between them becomes.

To make sure you understand, try the following problem and check the answer at the end of the chapter.

Wearing your bermuda shorts and pith helmet, you discover an ancient firepit in the center of the tipi ring which you are excavating. You carefully remove 10 grams of charcoal from the hearth, taking care not to contaminate it. Dropping the sample into the mail to Geochron Laboratories in Cambridge, Massachusetts, you decide to examine the artifacts. After you have counted some 4 million potsherds, the laboratory's answer arrives. Eagerly you rip open the envelope to see this: 3261 ±160.

What is the range in the limits of the date at the 68% level?_____

What about 95%? _____

99.74%? _____

Even though radiocarbon dating is a widely used method, it does have certain limitations. Because it is difficult to measure small quantities of beta emissions, this method can only be used for samples less than 50,000 years old.

Potassium-Argon Dating

At this point, it may be useful to discuss another method which relies upon the radioactive decay of elements. Potassium-argon dating works on the same principle as the carbon-14 method and uses ^{40}K and ^{40}A. This method allows us to go back much further in time; in fact, it is not useful for anything less than 1 million years old. The half-life for radioactive ^{40}K is 1.3 billion years. Thus, by comparing the amount of potassium in a sample to the amount of argon, the age of the sample can be determined. The most widely known use of this method occurred at Olduvai Gorge in Tanzania. Here, Louis Leakey uncovered the remains of *Australopithecus robustus* imbedded in volcanic ash. The K/A method revealed the lowest level of the site to be 1.75 million years old. Therefore, human paleontology was reexamined in the light of this new information. Certain precautions must also be noted in the use of this procedure. Rocks which are imported into a site cannot be relied upon for accurate information since they could quite possibly be millions of years older than the site itself. Thus only potassium-rich volcanic strata which were either deposited shortly before or after the period of human occupation can give an accurate reflection of the time perspective involved.

Paleomagnetic Dating

A more recent method of absolute dating, using paleomagnetism, has attempted to correlate the position of the earth's magnetic field and the alignment of iron particles in baked clay. Recorded observations over the last four hundred years have shown unpredictable changes in the positioning of the magnetic force field. Current research has focused on measuring the angle of declination between magnetic north and true north for various parts of the world. This knowledge is useful since other studies have demonstrated that the grains of hematite and magnetite in unfired clay occur in random positions. Once the clay is heated, these particles align themselves with the magnetic field. Upon cooling, this positioning is frozen. By measuring the angles of alignment and comparing them to the established charts, one can calculate the time of firing. Paleomagnetic dating can only be used on stationary objects, for example, the clay floor of a burned house. Even then, the clay square is carefully marked and treated before its removal from the field. This method is not useful in dating portable clay items, such as pottery, since they may have been traded over long distances. This makes the location of the object difficult to establish at the time of its firing. The initial work for paleomagnetic dating is conducted in the field, but the readings are obtained in the laboratory with the use of highly sensitive magnets. Such a technique holds much promise for the future dating of relevant archaeological and paleontological sites.

CONCLUSION

Before this discussion is terminated, a few more important points should be brought up. None of the above techniques would be possible without the acceptance of the principle of uniformitarianism. Simply stated, this means that processes which are presently occurring are assumed to have been operating in the past. This may seem to be an easy assumption to make, but it was more difficult to derive than you might expect. As the complexity of human culture increases, we find ourselves creating changes in nature. The atmospheric testing of nuclear bombs is an example. The calculated effects of this testing also had to be examined in the light of carbon-14 production. Only when these had been determined could the principle of uniformitarianism be put into action.

A second point we should take into consideration is the method of cross-dating, or using more than one technique for confirmation. No single dating technique should be used by itself. Anthropologists use a number of these techniques to check the reliability of their data. Relative dating may give us some clues which are unobtainable by absolute techniques, and the opposite is also true. All the evidence must be analyzed. If there is disagreement between conclusions, then other circumstances must be thoroughly investigated. Being a scientist does not mean that one simply goes into the field and collects data. A question must be asked before any answers can be ascertained. The problem of science is knowing which questions to ask. By having differing perceptions, scientists may be able to break through the barricades which limit our understanding.

A philosopher once made this point by telling the following story about physicist Ernst Mach. Supposedly, Mach was walking down the street when he noticed a man cleaning windows high above him. His attention was drawn by the man slipping on the window ledge. Suddenly the man's retaining belt broke and he began to fall toward the pavement. Horrified, and yet unable to turn away, Mach watched as the man came to the first story where an awning had been placed. The screaming window cleaner hit the canvas and flipped onto the sidewalk feet first. Somewhat dazed by his miraculous recovery, the man was startled when Mach ran up to him and asked, "When you were falling did you think you were moving toward the earth or that the ground was moving toward you?" Muttering obscenities, the window cleaner ran into the building.

Indeed, if this had happened to any of us, we may have had the same reaction as the window cleaner. But the point of the story is not its effect on the window cleaner, but the question posed by Mach. Some years later, this same question stimulated Einstein to invent the theory of relativity. Science is a process of asking questions. The collection of data is important only for testing the reliability of the solution.

Finally, we should mention that this examination of dating methods by no means exhausts the inventory of techniques available to the anthropologist. You may have already noticed that most of these methods were developed outside of the field of anthropology. For instance, the principle of stratigraphy comes from the field of geology, dendrochronology from forestry and astronomy, and radiocarbon dating from physics. Without an exchange of knowledge between different disciplines, little would have been accomplished. At the same time, we should remember the collection of data and the invention of theories by anthropologists may be useful to scholars in other fields. This scientific feedback from one discipline to another helps to bring about a more complete understanding of the world we live in.

EXERCISE: METHODS OF STRATIGRAPHIC INTERPRETATION AND RATE OF ACCUMULATION.

A. Examine the figure and answer the questions. Artifacts are represented by letters.

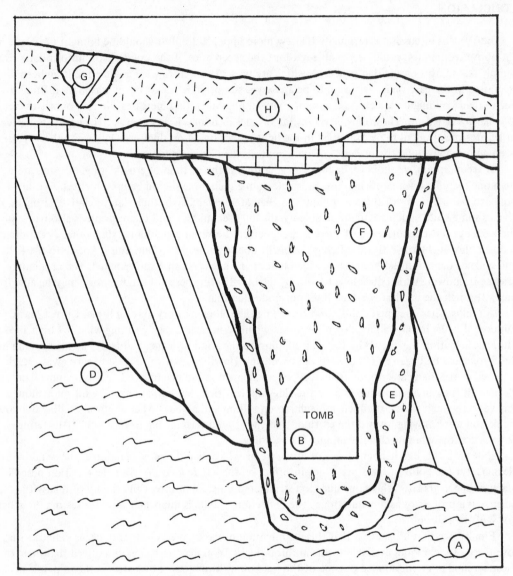

Stratigraphy at King Fufu's tomb.

1. There are four artifacts shown which are found in intrusive strata. These four are

    _____ , _____ , _____ , _____

2. Artifact D is a coin with a date corresponding to 100 B.C. Another coin, A, is dated at 300 B.C. Since there is a difference in the dates, A and D could not actually be in the same deposit, and therefore the stratigraphy must be corrected. (   ) True (   ) False

3. The evidence suggests that the makers of the tomb first dug into the gravel pit, placed the burial in the location shown, and then filled the pit with the gravel which might have filled it originally. (   ) True (   ) False

4. If one *did* accept the hypothesis given in question 3, then artifact F originally might have been deeper than either D or E. (   ) True   (   ) False
5. Note that D and E are at about the same depth. It is therefore more likely that D and E are stratigraphically contemporary than are D and A. (   ) True   (   ) False
6. Artifact B is deeper than D. It is therefore a sound conclusion that B was deposited before D. (   ) True   (   ) False
7. What is the best arrangement (oldest to youngest) of the artifacts G, C, F, A, and H? Place

    the oldest on the first of the blanks _____ , _____ , _____ , _____ , _____

B. Age estimates can sometimes be made by determining rates of accumulation. Let's use guano deposits to illustrate the idea.

   The cold Humbolt Current off the coast of Peru is rich in fish. Millions of predatory sea birds depend on the fish as food. The birds roost on the land, and their nitrate-abundant manure forms deep guano accumulations, which have commercial value as fertilizer. Presuming the average rate of deposition is 1 centimeter per 100 years, how old should an object be if it is two meters deep in bird droppings? What sort of errors might you anticipate?

_____

_____

_____

_____

_____

_____

_____

_____

_____

_____

_____

_____

_____

_____

Answers to problems on page 22:
   One standard deviation $\approx 68\%$ = 3101 to 3421
   Two standard deviations $\approx 95\%$ = 2941 to 3581
   Three standard deviations $\approx 99.74\%$ = 2781 to 3741

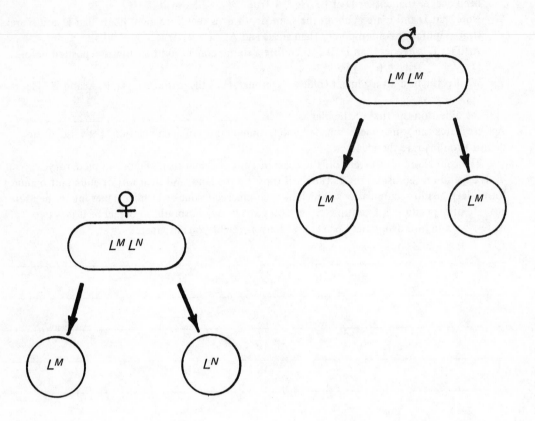

CHAPTER 3
Mechanisms of Evolution

Evolution is the change in the frequency of something through time. On this basis, all kinds of phenomena evolve: societies, molecules, organisms, and galaxies. Anthropologists focus their attention upon the evolution of humans, both culturally and biologically. Later in the chapter we will learn what it is that changes in frequency as a result of biological evolution. And, although our focus is biological, or organic, change, some of the processes of change are in fact analogous for cultural evolution as well.

There are four processes which create organic evolution: selection, mutation, drift, and nonrandom mating. It is vitally important to understand them, since they are essential to an explanation of the course of evolution.

BASIC CONCEPTS

Be sure you understand the meaning of *gene, allele, genotype, phenotype, mating type,* and *population structure.* The following definitions are given informally as aids in the discussion.

Genes are classes of hereditary units. For example, there is a gene which controls the type of ear wax (cerumen) which you have. Stick your finger in your ear (gently) and rub off some of the wax. If you have wet ear wax, it will have a slippery feel when rubbed between the fingers. Dry wax will crumble.

Why do some people have wet ear wax while others have dry wax? One answer is that the characteristic is under genetic control. There is a gene for the waxiness, and the particular kind of wax that any person has depends upon what happened to be inherited from the parents. The problem with this answer is that it begs the question, since one must then ask the same question about the parents, the parents' parents, and so on. To really answer the question, one would have to turn to an evolutionary explanation. This would involve some combination of selection, drift, nonrandom mating, and mutation. For the moment, recognize that the type of ear wax one has is a trait which is under genetic control and which exists in different varieties. In other words, it depends on genes.

An *allele* is a particular variety of a gene. Different kinds of ear wax are a result of different combinations of alleles. There may be any number of these. In the ABO blood types, for example, there is one allele for type A blood, one for type B, and another for type O. There are three alleles in this case, but some genes may have hundreds.

The term *phenotype* refers to the manifestation of genetic traits in an individual as opposed to that individual's actual genetic makeup. Recall that when Mendel bred his famous peas, one of the crosses was between pea plants with long stems and pea plants with short stems. All of the offspring had long stems even though they shared the genetic heritage of both long- and short-stemmed parents. Genetically, the offspring had alleles for both types of stem, but their appearance reflected only one of the parental stocks. Not all phenotypes are obvious; some can only be detected through laboratory tests. We all have numerous blood-group phenotypes, but they cannot be determined by a visual inspection. Think of a phenotype as the physical expression of a trait as opposed to a genotype, which is the genetic heritage of a trait.

Genotype refers to the actual combination of alleles in an individual. In a bisexual species (including ours), each individual receives two alleles, one of which came from each parent. Thus, although there may be several alleles for a given trait, the individual has only two of those alleles. For example, the genotype $I^O I^O$ represents one individual of blood type O in the ABO blood group. Other possible genotypes would be $I^A I^A$, $I^A I^O$, $I^B I^B$, $I^B I^O$, and $I^A I^B$. Note that the alleles that affect the trait may be the same (as in $I^A I^A$) or different (as in $I^A I^O$). If both alleles are the same, the individual is said to be homozygous. If the alleles are contrasting, the individual is said to be heterozygous. A homozygous individual receives the same kind of allele from each parent; the heterozygous individual receives a different allele from each parent. Determine for yourself which of the genotypes listed for the ABO blood group are homozygous and which are heterozygous.

A *mating type* is the cross between two individuals' genotypes. To illustrate this, let's examine another blood group system, the MN system, which is independent of the ABO group. There are two alleles: L^M and L^N. There are three genotypes: L^ML^M, L^ML^N, and L^NL^N. These are the ways that individual people would be represented. To indicate a mating type, we need to show a cross between two people. This is done by marking an X between them. If one L^ML^M homozygote were mated to an L^ML^N heterozygote, the mating type would be $L^ML^M \times L^ML^N$. Remember: It takes two alleles to make one genotype, and two genotypes to make one mating type. Determine all of the possible mating types in the MN system.

_____

_____

_____

The answer is at the end of the chapter.

Population structure refers to the arrangement of alleles, genotypes, and mating types in a population. In one population, for example, an allele might have a frequency of 0.6, while it is 0.4 in another. In short, populations differ in the frequency of alleles. They may also differ in a frequency of genotypes and mating types. They may differ in the proportion of genotypes and mating types even if they have the same frequencies for alleles. One thus describes the population structure of a group by determining the frequency of different alleles, genotypes, and mating types which the population has. We began by defining evolution as a change in the frequency of "something." More precisely, organic evolution is the systematic change in the population structure.

PREDICTING OFFSPRING GENOTYPE

Let's consider the facts of life. Typical body cells have a pair of alleles for each genetic trait. But, each reproductive cell (sperm in men and ova in women) contains only one allele of any given gene, and the offspring receive one allele from each parent. This process by which one member of each pair of corresponding alleles separates from the other is called *meiosis*. At fertilization, each allele from each parent combines to make an individual with two alleles for each trait.

In figure 3.1, observe how the alleles segregate in a male of genotype L^ML^M and a female of genotype L^ML^N.

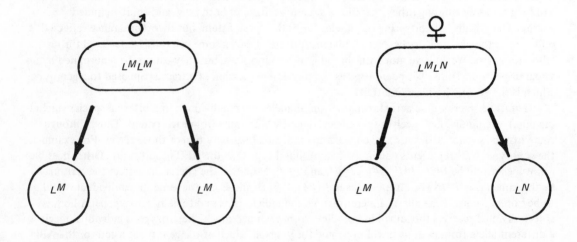

Figure 3.1.

Each single allele will be part of a sex cell and each member of the pair of alleles is represented in 50% of the reproductive cells. Either of the sperm could combine with either of the eggs. It is a random occurrence (unless certain types of selection interfere).

To determine the predicted frequency of the offspring genotypes, you can use the roman, or Punnett, square you probably learned in the ninth grade. Draw a square with four cells. On the vertical axis, place the two alleles which one parent could transmit. Place the other parent's alleles on the horizontal axis. Then write each combination in the appropriate cell.

The mating type $L^ML^M \times L^ML^N$ is shown in figure 3.2.

	L^M	L^N
L^M	L^ML^M	L^ML^N
L^M	L^ML^M	L^ML^N

Figure 3.2.

The next step is to count the number of different combinations. In this case there are two: homozygous L^ML^M genotypes and heterozygous L^ML^N genotypes. Count the frequency of each genotype. Here, the expected proportion of the children is 50% of each. By using the square, you can predict that half of the offspring are expected to be L^ML^M and the other half are expected to be L^ML^N.

Confirm your mastery of the square by crossing these:

1. $L^ML^M \times L^ML^M$
2. $L^ML^N \times L^ML^N$

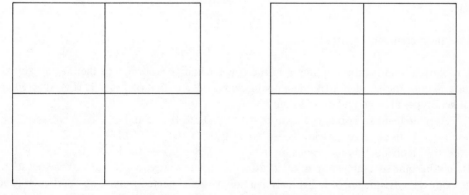

The outcome of the first is 100% L^ML^M. For the second, it is 25% L^ML^M + 50% L^ML^N + 25% L^NL^N. Stop and obtain help if you did not get the correct answers.

Be aware that the process gives the theoretical expectation. Certain mechanisms of evolution (such as mutation and selection) can affect the outcome before the person is born. Recognize that the outcome is a matter of probability—not certainty. If we had four children from the mating type $L^ML^N \times L^ML^N$, we would expect one-fourth to be L^NL^N. With such a small sample, however, it is quite possible to find none of this genotype. On the other hand, we might find any number between one and four.

HARDY-WEINBERG EQUILIBRIUM

Mendel's laws are used to predict the genotypes of individuals. A different principle applies to populations. The theory behind it was independently described by Hardy (an English mathematician) and Weinberg (a German physician). Incidentally, German speakers refer to it as the Weinberg-Hardy law. Either way, the description was first made in order to show that so-called dominant alleles do not become more common than recessive alleles merely because one is dominant and one is recessive. (These terms do not apply if the heterozygote can be distinguished from both homozygotes.)

In one sense, the law is quite trivial. It states that the genetic structure does not change unless some mechanism of evolution makes it change. This is not as simple as it sounds, since it enables scientists to compare a theoretical expectation to what is actually observed in a population. Only populations evolve. Individual people grow, develop, and change, but they do not become different organisms.

Let's begin with the mechanics of the law and then discuss some applications. We will examine only the simple case of one gene which has two alleles, A and a. The frequency of A is designated with the symbol p, while q is used for the frequency of a.

The sum of the frequencies of the two alleles is equal to unity: $p + q = 1$. In other words, if p has a frequency of 0.7 in a population, and if q has a frequency of 0.3, then the total of p and q is the whole (unity, one, or 100%).

A population has genotypes produced by the combination of alleles. What types could occur? One possibility is to obtain two A's together (AA). Another is with two a's (aa). The third is with an A and an a (Aa). There are no others. We could therefore write a simple formula for the frequencies of genotypes as follows: $pp + pq + qq = 1$.

The sum of the different genotypes will equal the total number of individuals in the population (for this particular group of alleles).

Now comes a slight complication. There is only one way to become a homozygote. Both parents must contribute the same allele. There are two ways to become a heterozygote. Either parent could give either an A or an a. Thus, in regard to the frequency of genotypes expected in a population, we must multiply the frequency of the heterozygotes by two. The frequencies are expressed by the formula:

$$pp + 2pq + qq = 1$$

or, in the most commonly written form:

$$p^2 + 2pq + q^2 = 1$$

If evolution is not happening, the frequencies will combine according to the formula above. To illustrate, assume the frequency of p in a population is 0.2 and that of q is 0.8. The expected proportion of genotypes in the population is then:

Individuals homozygous for $p = p^2 = 0.2 \times 0.2 = 0.04$
Heterozygous individuals $= 2pq = 2(0.2 \times 0.8) = 2(0.16) = 0.32$
Individuals homozygous for $q = q^2 = 0.8 \times 0.8 = 0.64$

Do not become so wrapped up in calculating the answer that you lose track of the question. The results express the frequency of individuals in a population expected to have any particular genotype relative to the frequency of alleles in the population. For the example above, 32% are expected to be heterozygotes if $p = 20\%$ and $q = 80\%$.

Now consider the converse. Suppose we wish to describe a group by allelic frequency and we know the proportion of genotypes. As long as all three genotypes can be recognized (no dominance is involved), this is a simple matter of direct counting. Note that some of the A alleles in the group belong to the AA homozygotes. The remainder belong to the Aa heterozygotes. The same circumstance applies also to the a allele. Heterozygotes have equal numbers of A and a alleles. Write the formulas for determining the frequencies of A and a (p and q) in the space below.

$p =$
$q =$

Could you do it? If not, check the answer at the end of the chapter.

If one allele is dominant to the other, the allelic frequencies must be estimated instead of being counted. Let's say A is dominant to a. The AA homozygotes and the Aa heterozygotes would then share the same phenotype, and we could not tell them apart. Yet we do know the frequency for the homozygous recessive aa genotype, q^2, and this is sufficient to solve the problem, or at least estimate the answer on the presumption of equilibrium. This is done by taking the square root of the latter, and then subtracting this number, q, from unity to obtain the frequency p.

$$q = \sqrt{q^2}$$
$$p = 1 - q$$

To illustrate with the numbers already given, $q = \sqrt{0.64} = 0.8$. Since there are only two alleles, p must represent the remainder: $1 - 0.8 = 0.2$.

We now turn to applying the equilibrium theory in order to analyze evolution. Suppose we want to know whether evolution is affecting a genetic trait. The Hardy-Weinberg law tells us the proportion of genotypes to anticipate if no mechanisms of evolution are operating. Logically, therefore, we could compare the expected proportion to what is actually observed.

The MN blood groups have been previously mentioned. They are again used as an example. Assume we typed the blood of 1000 people in a population and discovered that 20% were $L^M L^M$, 60% were $L^M L^N$, and 20% were $L^N L^N$. First, calculate the frequency of alleles. In this case, $L^M = 20\% + 60\% \div 2 = 50\%$. $L^N = 20\% + 60\% \div 2 = 50\%$. Given these frequencies, what are the expected proportions of genotypes if evolutionary mechanisms are not operating? The formula for Hardy-Weinberg equilibrium gives the answer.

Expected	Actually Observed
$L^M L^M = 0.5^2 = 0.25$	$L^M L^M = 0.20$
$L^M L^N = 2(0.5 \times 0.5) = 0.50$	$L^M L^N = 0.60$
$L^N L^N = 0.5^2 = 0.25$	$L^N L^N = 0.20$

Note that in this case the theoretical numbers do not match the observed numbers. There are 10% more heterozygotes than expected, while each of the homozygotic classes have 5% less than expected. On what basis was the prediction made? That's correct—the prediction assumed that evolution was not affecting the particular trait for this particular group. Yet, if the actual observations are different from this presumption, our only conclusion can be that some mechanisms of evolution are operating. We also know the magnitude of the consequence.

What we do not know is which evolutionary mechanism causes the change. It may also be a particular combination of factors. Ascertaining this answer requires additional knowledge and advanced methods. The important thing is to understand how hypotheses can be obtained in order to explain the difference. One possible answer is that natural selection favors the heterozygotes. Perhaps some of the homozygotes are being spontaneously aborted before birth. This spontaneous abortion could be the reason that fewer of them are present than expected. Perhaps the population is not mating at random.

A problem thus exists for which all possible solutions must be tested empirically. New discoveries are often made in the pursuit of answers to such problems. Science is a matter of putting a puzzle together when some of the pieces are missing and on one knows how many pieces there are or even what the puzzle will be like when it's finished. For that matter, no one knows if the puzzle is ever finished.

The pieces are put together by following rules of relationships. For the evolutionary answer, one must demonstrate how the mechanisms of evolution operate to give any particular result. Each of these will be briefly discussed so that you will have a general idea about how they change the population structure.

We will ruthlessly ignore any complications to focus on the general idea. To help us, the people of Popo volunteer their population structure. They are a rather odd group since there are only six of the Popo, they only have one gene, and this gene has but two varieties: a^1 and a^2. Note that the numbers next to a are superscripts rather than exponents.

DRIFT

First examine figure 3.3. It represents a Popo village and contains six individuals. Calculate the allelic frequencies. Note that direct counting will enable you to do this. There are six a^1 alleles and six a^2 alleles, so the original frequency of both is 50%.

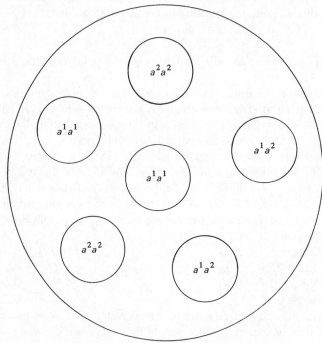

Figure 3.3. Population structure among the Popo.

What happens if some of the Popo move to a new location? If all of them go, they will carry with them all of the alleles in the entire group. If only some of them go, there is a chance that not all of the alleles will be represented among the migrants. The smaller the migrating sample is, the less likely it is that all of the alleles will be represented in the original 50% proportion. Small populations are particularly influenced by random fluctuations.

Let's sort people randomly into mating pairs, and send them off to found a new village in a different location. One way to simulate this is by tossing coins. Let a^1 represent heads and a^2 represent tails. Toss two coins together to represent one individual. Note the resulting combination.

To illustrate: Suppose the first toss gave two heads together (a^1a^1). This person needs a mate. Suppose the next toss again gave two heads (another a^1a^1). Now send this happily mated pair to their new home (see figure 3.4).

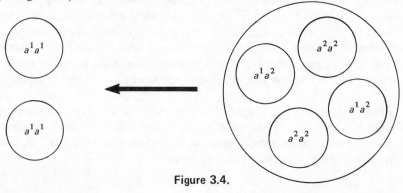

Figure 3.4.

Next, compare the genetic structure in the two villages and observe how the distribution of the variation has changed. The new village has 100% a^1, and the old village has 25% a^1 and 75% a^2. Also note that the distribution of genotypes and potential mating types is different.

Try this yourself four times and mark the different combinations below.

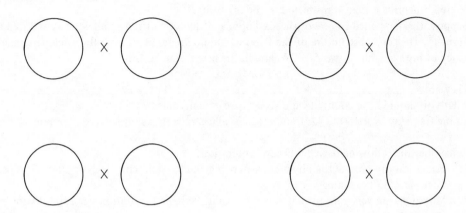

Were all of your combinations of two the same? Were all of them representative of the 50% frequencies from which they were drawn?

Probably there were differences in some of your trials. As the mating pairs produce children, such different combinations will be continued through time. This has happened simply on the basis of accident.

Having small groups of migrants which are not representative of the original group in every single gene is thus one way in which populations can become different. We can obtain a similar result with no migration at all. Anything that decimates a population to a small size will have the same effect. Pestilence, famine, and war have often reduced large groups to a few survivors. Even if the deaths are random, the survivors may not have the same genetic structure as before the disaster.

Return to figure 3.3. Flip two coins again and observe the combination. Find the person matching the combination at the Popo village and rub him out. Placing a coin over the appropriate circle is convenient. Continue the disaster until only two survivors remain. Do these two survivors match the frequency of alleles which previously existed? As you can see, they may not.

Remember these basic facts about drift.
1. It is strictly random, and the only cause is accident.
2. Drift is important only when populations are small especially when they are less than one hundred mating pairs.
3. Until a few thousand years ago, human populations were small. Some remain so even today. Under these conditions, accident can account for some of the differences which we see among populations.

MUTATION

Mutation directly affects the structure of the individual genes by altering them to a new physical form. Sometimes entire chromosomes can be affected, but we will discuss only the most simple mutations. Genes are a blueprint ordering the kinds of biochemical reactions which occur within the body. Suppose you were to construct an elaborate model of a house by making it out of Tinker Toys. You could then give the model to someone with instructions to follow the design. The same design could be used to produce any number of identical houses. The constancy would depend on the design remaining the same.

Mutation is analogous to shooting the model with a rifle. Sometimes the bullet might pass through without striking a piece. Sometimes it would completely destroy it. Radiation can do this to the very tiny and complicated genes. Cosmic rays, for example, will penetrate biological tissue as if nothing were there. They travel at the speed of light and have enormous force compared to the miniscule genetic particles. Radiation will sometimes strike the sex cells and change the heredity blueprint. The altered blueprint is then transmitted to the offspring.

Suppose this happened to one of the six Popo, and that one of the a^2 alleles was mutated to the new form a^3. The genetic structure of the Popo would no longer be exactly the same. Originally, the frequency of both a^1 and a^2 was 50%. What will the new frequencies be?

They are _____ %a^1, _____ %a^2, and _____ %a^3.
What you should have counted were six a^1, five a^2, and one a^3.
So the frequencies are 50%, 42%, and 8%. The allele a^2 is thus no longer as common as it once was.

Remember the following basic facts about mutation.
1. Radiation can change the physical form of a gene. (Certain chemicals and other processes might also do the same.)
2. Mutations are very rare for individual sex cells. Perhaps 1 mutation per 100,000 nonmutations is a reasonable average.
3. Mutation by itself is not important to the changing of genetic structure, because the events are so rare.
4. However, it is the *only* way in which new kinds of genes are produced. All other mechanisms of evolution only alter the frequency of what already existed. Life as we know it would be impossible if mutation never happened.

SELECTION

Suppose the Popo were exposed to some particular disease. The presence of a^1 conferred immunity; those without it contracted the disease and died before producing children. Return to figure 3.3, and note that there are two Popo which do lack a^1. Eliminate the two a^2a^2 homozygotes and recalculate the frequencies among the four survivors.

a^1 = _____ % a^2 = _____ %

Since two of the survivors are a^1a^1 and two are a^1a^2, the changed frequencies are 75% and 25% respectively.

Recognize the point. Alleles are being systematically selected instead of taken at random. The consequence will be that one form will become more common through time while another will become less common. This phenomenon was first discovered by Darwin and Wallace and is responsible for most of the evolutionary change which results in different kinds of species.

You might wish to try the same simulation through several generations. Cross the survivors at random to produce offspring. Subject them to the same selection. Note the third, fourth, and fifth generation frequencies. Plot the frequencies on a piece of paper. Connect the dots. What is the shape of the line you obtain? Is it curved rather than straight? Can you explain why? What do you conclude about the kind of systematic change that happens?

Remember the following basic facts about selection.
1. It is systematic and not random.
2. Ordinarily, selection is not very strong. An evolutionary change of about 1% in 10,000 years is actually rather fast.
3. Mutation and selection operate together to produce equilibrium values dependent upon the strength of both.

NONRANDOM MATING

The consequence of nonrandom mating does not happen until the following generation. To simulate it therefore, we must nonrandomly cross the mating pairs and then compare the offspring to the parents.

Whenever anything is randomly selected, it has a probability of being chosen which depends solely upon its frequency in a set. For the Popo, we took equal starting frequencies for both alleles. Since the frequency of a^1 is 0.5, the odds of randomly obtaining two a^1a^1 together are (0.5 × 0.5) × (0.5 × 0.5) or the frequency of a^1 to the fourth power or 0.0625. You need to know the following general rule of probability: *To calculate the probability of independent events randomly occurring together, multiply their individual frequencies.*

Thus, if the frequency of any particular event is 1 in 10, the probability of it happening 3 times in a row or 3 times together is (0.1)(0.1)(0.1) or 0.1^3 or 0.001 or 1 in 1000.

Let's apply the rule to ascertain the random expectation for mating types. First, write down the mating type. Second, write down the frequency of each allele for the entire mating type.

Third, if the mating includes heterozygous genotypes, double their frequency since there are two ways to be heterozygous. Finally, multiply the frequencies of the two genotypes together.

As an example, let's look at the mating type $a^1a^1 \times a^1a^2$.

$$(.5)(.5) \times 2\ [(.5)(.5)]$$
$$= .25 \times 2(.25)$$
$$= .1250 \text{ or } 12\frac{1}{2}\%$$

Take the mating type $a^1a^2 \times a^1a^2$ with $a^1 = 0.6$ and $a^2 = 0.4$. Write the expected frequency below.

Frequency of $a^1a^2 \times a^1a^2$ =

Refer to the answer at the end of the chapter to verify.

This is a way to determine whether a population is mating at random for any given mating type. One merely needs to compare the expected frequency of occurrence to the frequencies which are actually observed in a population.

To demonstrate nonrandom mating, we will take a case in which individuals deliberately select their mates. Assume that everyone chooses someone with an identical genotype. Again refer to figure 3.3, and determine how many possible mating types there would be if this were to happen.

The possible mating types are:

_____

_____

The answer is that only three kinds of mating would happen if like were mated only to like: $a^1a^1 \times a^1a^1$, $a^1a^2 \times a^1a^2$, and $a^2a^2 \times a^2a^2$.

The next step is to determine what kind of offspring would result from these three mating types. To keep the numbers simple, assume that each mating type has four children. The expected proportion of the offspring are as follows:

Mating Type 1	Mating Type 2	Mating Type 3
$a^1a^1 \times a^1a^1$	$a^1a^2 \times a^1a^2$	$a^2a^2 \times a^2a^2$
$4\,a^1a^1$	$1\,a^1a^1,\ 2\,a^1a^2,\ 1\,a^2a^2$	$4\,a^2a^2$

Do these children have the same genotypic ratios as existed among their parents? There is an easy way to find out. Count the number of children of each genotype. There is a total of five a^1a^1 offspring, there are two a^1a^2, and five a^2a^2. Since we stipulated that each mating type has four children, the second generation consists of twelve individuals. Divide the number of each genotype by twelve, and we have the frequency in the second generation. Doing this, we obtain 42% a^1a^1, 16% a^1a^2, and 42% a^2a^2, whereas random mating with the same starting frequency of alleles being 50% produces children in the ratio: 25% a^1a^1, 50% a^1a^2, and 25% a^2a^2.

Note that the second generation differs from the first in the genotypic ratios, and that this has occurred by nonrandom assortment.

Remember these basic facts about nonrandom mating.
1. It alters the proportion of genotypes.
2. It can alter genotypic frequencies drastically in a single generation; thus it is a strong evolutionary mechanism.
3. A tendency for like genotypes to mate together is called positive assortative mating.

We used positive assortative mating as an example of nonrandom mating. Its effect is to increase the proportion of homozygotes in the next generation. The converse circumstance is when unlike genotypes mate together more commonly than expected at random. This is negative assortative mating. It increases the frequency of heterozygotes in the next generation.

In actuality, population structure is never as simple as our imaginary case of the Popo. There are about 4 billion people in the world. No one knows how many human genes there are; one conservative estimate is 30,000. Some of these probably have hundreds of alleles. No one can decide how many different populations exist. At least 2000 ethnic groups are recognized by anthropologists, and smaller divisions are possible. Furthermore, mechanisms of evolution do not occur in isolation; they combine on a scale of infinite proportions. Despite this enormous complexity in natural populations, the principles of evolutionary change are the same for all peoples and species.

EXERCISE: GENETICS PROBLEMS

1. Brachydactyly is a disorder in which the fingers and toes are abnormally short. It is caused by a dominant allele, B. The allele for normal fingers and toes is b. A person has brachydactyly whenever B occurs in their genotype. In the mating type $Bb \times bb$, what percentage of the children are expected to have the disorder?

2. A gene designated C has two alleles: C^w and C^r. C^w has a frequency of 0.9 and C^r of 0.1. What is the expected frequency of C^rC^r homozygotes in the population?

3. The following frequencies of genotypes have been observed: T^xT^x, 20%; T^xT^z, 38%; T^zT^z, 42%. What is the frequency of T^x and T^z?

4. Given the frequency of alleles for the problem above, what are the genotypic ratios if the population is in Hardy-Weinberg equilibrium?

5. Assume the frequency of allele A is 0.6 and the frequency of a is 0.4. If random mating is present, what is the frequency of the mating type $AA \times aa$?

6. There is a theory called Wahlund's principle which is usually taught in advanced classes of population genetics. We believe you can deduce the general idea on the basis of applying what you have learned. Here is the problem.

    All the women on the University Frisbee Team select their mates from the Beaver Club. The Frisbee Team and the Beaver Club are not exactly the same biologically. The alleles for a gene Z have these frequencies:

    In the Frisbee Team: $Z^1 = 0.6$ and $Z^2 = 0.4$
    In the Beaver Club: $Z^1 = 0.4$ and $Z^2 = 0.6$

A. What are the zygotic ratios among the Frisbee Beaver kids?

B. How do these ratios among the children compare to what would be the case with mating if both organizations were genetically isolated?

C. Describe in your own words what happens to zygotic ratios when two different populations merge together.

Hint: The heterozygosity in the merged population is 52% (Z^1 in Frisbee Team $\times$ Z^2 in Beaver Club + Z^2 in Frisbee Team $\times$ Z^1 in Beaver Club).

Answers to problems on pages 29, 30, and 35:

Page 29: With two alleles L^M and L^N, there are nine possible mating types. Some of them, however, are reciprocals.

$L^M L^M \times L^M L^M$	$L^M L^N \times L^M L^M$	$L^N L^N \times L^M L^M$
$L^M L^M \times L^M L^N$	$L^M L^N \times L^M L^N$	$L^N L^N \times L^M L^N$
$L^M L^M \times L^N L^N$	$L^M L^N \times L^N L^N$	$L^N L^N \times L^N L^N$

Page 30: The formula for determining the frequencies of p and q if no dominance is involved is:

$$p = \overline{AA} + \overline{Aa}/2$$
$$q = \overline{aa} + \overline{Aa}/2$$

in which the bars refer to the frequency of genotypes. You might have used some other symbol.

Page 35: If mating occurs at random for $a^1 a^2 \times a^1 a^2$, and if $a^1 = .6$ while $a^2 = .4$, then the mating type happens at the frequency:

$$2(a^1 a^2) \times 2(a^1 a^2)$$
$$= 2(.6 \times .4) \times 2(.6 \times .4)$$
$$= .2304$$

FLAKING METHODS

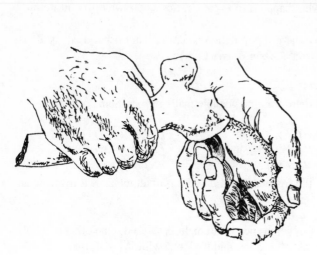

SOFT HAMMER

HAMMER STONE

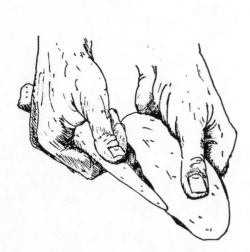

PRESSURE FLAKING

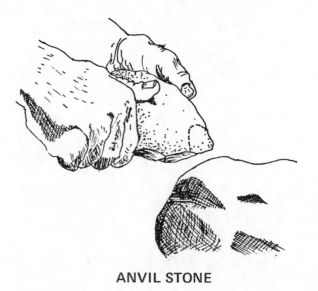

ANVIL STONE

CHAPTER 4
Early Human Tools

A few species of animals, other than humans, are sometimes known to use tools. Birds and sea otters, for example, have been seen to crack shellfish with stones. Chimpanzees have been observed to use leaves as sponges to obtain water from tree hollows. The most sophisticated use of tools among nonhumans under natural conditions occurs when chimpanzees modify the shape of sticks and insert them into termite nests. During certain times of the year, termites will climb onto the stick, which is then withdrawn by the chimp to collect the juicy insects.

The earliest human tools must certainly have been objects at hand—sticks, rocks, and bones. As time progressed, people learned how to make them more efficient for desired purposes, such as cutting, chopping, hammering, and digging. An important point to recognize is that the toolmaker had to form a mental concept or visualization of how to make the desired object from the raw material. The method of manufacture would be influenced by the individual's knowledge, experience, and cultural tradition.

In the exercise in this chapter, you will manufacture stone tools yourself. However, our first goal is to provide you with some familiarity with the way anthropologists organize the archaeological record. The film *Early Stone Tools* demonstrates some of the manufacturing techniques used by primitive technologists. Making a specimen for yourself will increase your appreciation of the processes required to produce a primitive artifact from a rock.

THE EVOLUTIONARY SEQUENCE

Let us review the major stages of prehistoric human development. Archaeologists often divide the record for early humans into the Paleolithic, Mesolithic, and Neolithic. The Neolithic marks the rise of food production with the domestication of plants and animals. It is characterized by farming and village life. The Mesolithic is a transitional stage between food gathering and farming. It is most clearly distinguished in Europe, where Mesolithic sites often include very tiny flakes of stone called microliths. For the rest of the Old World, the Mesolithic is not as clearly defined; in fact, many archaeologists do not use the term. We will focus on the Paleolithic and especially on tools made of stone. Remember, however, that other materials were almost certainly just as important (if not more so) in the daily lives of the people. The great proportion of stone items from the Paleolithic is largely a function of the permanence of the raw material; artifacts made from perishable substances are less often preserved for our record.

Traditionally, the Paleolithic is divided into three parts: the Lower, Middle, and Upper. In table 4.1, these are listed along with their approximate age, associated hominids, and some examples of toolmaking traditions. Observe that the biological and archaeological stages do not correspond exactly. The tools made by *Australopithecus* and *Homo erectus* both belong to the Lower Paleolithic. Neanderthals and early modern humans are associated with the Middle and Upper Paleolithic respectively.

PALEOLITHIC TOOL TYPES

Once a knapper (the toolmaker) selects a rock of appropriate material, he has a choice of two approaches to making a tool. He can either remove small pieces (flakes) from the core and work the flakes into a tool, or he can use the core itself.

Cores are large pieces of stone from which flakes have been removed. There are two basic types—bifacially worked cores and unifacially worked cores. The former are artifacts which have been flaked on both surfaces. Hand axes and chopping tools are examples of this type. Unifacially worked cores have been flaked on only one surface. Choppers are representative of this type.

The illustrations on the preceding page were redrawn from F. Clark Howell, *Early Man* (New York: Time-Life Books, 1965), pp. 110-11.

TABLE 4.1
Archaeological Stages in the Paleolithic

DIVISION	YEARS AGO	HOMINIDS	TRADITIONS
Upper	40,000	*H. s. sapiens*	Aurignacoid
Middle	150,000	*H. s. neanderthalensis*	Fauresmith Mousterian Sangoan
Lower		*H. erectus*	Clactonian Acheulean Abbevillian Chopper-chopping
	c. 2,000,000	*Australopithecus*	Oldowan Osteodontokeratic

The fragments of stone struck from a core are called flakes. Tools of this category tend to be more diversified and specialized than core tools. Flake tools are made by removing the outer portions of the core and are less than half as long as they are wide. Blank flakes are usually reworked to obtain the desired implement. Blades are parallel-sided flakes removed from the core by means of a punch. Blades are more than half as long as they are wide. This tool industry is characteristic of the Upper Paleolithic. The cores from which blades are taken are distinctive because of their prismatic shape.

METHODS OF KNAPPING

Direct percussion is a method used by a knapper to remove flakes from a core in which the knapper strikes the core directly with a hammer of stone, bone, antler, or wood. Sometimes an anvil may be used in conjunction with or instead of the hammer. This technique is used primarily to detach crude flakes and to trim cores.

Indirect percussion is similar to direct percussion with one exception. Instead of striking the core directly, the knapper uses a punch to direct the blow of the hammer more accurately. This permits the toolmaker to exert more control.

Pressure-flaking techniques are used for secondary chipping. Although occasionally found in the Middle Paleolithic, this method is most commonly associated with the Upper Paleolithic. Pressure flaking requires the use of softer or more elastic implements (such as an antler flaker). These are used to press off flakes rather than to strike them off.

PALEOLITHIC TRADITIONS

The conclusions concerning the first tradition we shall examine are somewhat speculative. No stone tools have been found in association with *Ramapithecus*. An examination of the hand of *Australopithecus* readily reveals its ability to manipulate tools. The paleontologist Raymond Dart has argued that these early hominids probably first used materials such as bones, teeth, and horns to make tools. He has called this tradition the Osteodontokeratic industry. Don't let the length of this term throw you; breaking it down into its constituent components, we find that *osteo* means bone, *donto* means teeth, and *kerato* means horn. Such tools were probably quite crude, but at the very least, they were essential for survival. Dart's evidence for this tradition is based on observations such as baboon skulls with depressions on their foreheads or frontal bones. Upon looking closer at these battered regions, Dart has concluded that they may have been made by the distal end of an antelope humerus. Hence, he believes *Australopithecus* must have used these foreleg bones as clubs in at least three sites. Some anthropologists reject this evidence as inconclusive.

The first stone artifacts are known as pebble tools. Often referred to as Oldowan, these bifacially worked core tools may have been invented to make different tools from wood or some other perishable material. It is possible they were also used to break open bones. Oldowan pebble tools are important since they provided the foundation for later stone toolmaking traditions.

In Africa and Europe, we see a gradual change in the frequency of core tools. Toward the Upper Paleolithic, a general decrease occurs. In contrast, flake tools become more abundant and slowly replace the core implements. The most common core tool is the hand axe. Invented in Africa, it gradually spread throughout most of western Europe and to parts of southwestern Asia. Basically, hand axes are bifacially worked tools and have a continuous sharp edge around the lower circumference. The upper portion is held in the user's hand; the tool can be used to cut, scrape, dig, or hammer.

An oval- or pear-shaped outline is characteristic of the earliest hand axes. Another distinguishing feature is an uneven or zigzag cutting edge. These early hand axes are representative of a stage of development referred to as *Abbevillian* after a *Homo erectus* site (Abbeville) located in southern France. The second stage of the Lower Paleolithic hand-axe industry is known as *Acheulean*, again named for a French site (St. Acheul). These pointed or almond-shaped hand axes are still a general-purpose tool. Cleavers, chipped stone balls, an occasional flake implement, wooden spears, throwing sticks, and clubs are all part of the Acheulean inventory. But the predominant tool of these early human populations is the hand axe, and it remains so for thousands of years.

An early European flake industry is represented by the Clactonian tradition of England. Flakes were first removed from one side of a core. Then the resulting scars were used as striking platforms to obtain larger and better-shaped flakes. The Clactonian tradition was short-lived and eventually absorbed by the Acheulean. From this source, a number of Acheulean tool users independently developed a second method for the production of flake tools. Known as the Levalloisian, this technique required a more sophisticated striking platform to be made on the core. By preparing this platform, the knapper could exercise more control over the size and shape of the flakes. The prepared core is patch-marked with flake scars, and the resulting appearance has reminded some specialists of an inverted tortoise shell. Once the desired flake is removed, its dome-shaped profile is quite similar to a small, flat hand axe. As a general rule, these flake tools were not worked to any great extent once separated from the core. Since most of the resulting tools seem to have functioned as skinning knives and scrapers, they may have been invented by cultures adapting to new hunting conditions in cold or wet environments.

In eastern Asia a somewhat different tool tradition (Chopper-chopping) is associated with the sites of the Lower Paleolithic. As in the West, this tradition produces multi-purpose tools, lasts throughout the Paleolithic, and finds core tools being gradually replaced by flake implements. Although the terms *chopper* and *chopping* may seem to indicate the same type of tool, there are basic differences. A chopper is a unifacially chipped core tool used primarily for scraping hides and other materials. A chopping tool is also shaped from a core, but it is worked on both surfaces, making it useful for cutting and slicing.

During late Lower and early Middle Paleolithic times, *Homo erectus* populations gradually evolve into Neanderthal groups (*Homo sapiens neanderthalensis*). Like the changes occurring in human morphological characteristics, the transition in lithic technology was a gradual one built upon the foundation of preceding centuries. A derivation of the Clactonian-Levalloisian sequence, and highly influenced by the Acheulean, the European-North African-Southwest Asiatic tradition is referred to as the Mousterian. The Mousterian, however, was not a uniform tradition, for regional variations have been detected. Along the river systems one form of the Mousterian is represented mostly by flake tools such as side scrapers, knives, and points (which may have been hafted to spears). A coastal variant includes a small number of hand axes along with flake tools. In addition to this geographical separation, there was also a temporal variation. The inland regions seem to have been occupied more during glacial times, while the coastal rim was more important during more temperate interglacial periods. During the interim, there was some intermixing between these two variants. As a reflection of the European Neanderthal's economy, we may point out that the inland, glacial cultures were probably more dependent on the hunting of large game animals than the coastal groups, who relied more on collecting their food resources.

Regional variation also existed among the communities of African Neanderthals. To the east and south, an arid and open savannah country is occupied by the Fauresmith assemblage. The most distinctive artifact of this industry is a relatively small (sometimes heart-shaped) hand axe commonly made of slate. A dense forest, requiring a different adaptation, reigned in the central portion of the continent. Picks, cleavers, and crude hand axes were associated with the Sangoan toolmakers who ex- ploited these groves.

The chopper-chopping tradition with a numerous variety of flake tools continues in Asia during this period. It lasts well into the European Upper Paleolithic. In some Asian localities, hand axes begin to appear slightly before the transition to the European Mesolithic. This is not to imply that the inhabitants of this region were more primitive. Indeed, present evidence indicates the contrary.

About 40,000 years ago the continual interchange between culture, biology, and environment began to result in some new forces appearing in the archaeological record. A new form of hominid gradually emerges and with it a new technological innovation (the blade traditions) can be ascertained. The earliest blade industries occur quite early (c. 75,000 years ago) in Libya and Israel, but then suddenly disappear, only to reemerge at about the same time as the first European traditions. At the present time, we are unable to locate the exact place or places of origin for this new method of tool- making. Moreover, the amount of regional variation within a single tradition was far greater than ever before.

Because of the wide variation in time and space found among the blade traditions of the world, we shall focus on a single sequence: the Dordogne of central France.

TABLE 4.2
The Dordogne Sequence of Blade Traditions
(Late Upper Pleistocene)

TRADITION	YEARS AGO
Magdalenian	10,000 to 21,000
Solutrean	15,000 to 22,000
Aurignacian	21,000 to 34,000
Perigordian	23,000 to 37,000

After Braidwood (1967).

From table 4.2 you should be able to see there is a great deal of overlap. This overlapping repre- sents, to some degree, the local variation found in just this region of France. For the country as a whole, an archaeologist would have five or six different sequences to discuss.

Rather than a detailed description of each of these traditions, only a broad outline will be given. You may want to refresh your memory about the production of blades by turning back to the sec- tion on Paleolithic tool types. The economies of all Upper Paleolithic cultures were based on hunting and gathering. Since the distribution of exploited resources only rarely permitted permanent villages to be maintained, most groups were nomadic. Group solidarity was maintained by kinship ties, the sharing of food, and probably by holding certain rituals or ceremonies.

A number of implements were made of bone. One of the more important inventions during this stage was the atlatl (spear thrower), which allowed a human being to increase the amount of thrust behind a projectile. Engraved atlatls (and indeed the most elaborate bone tools, such as barbed harpoons of decorated antler) are associated with the Magdalenian tradition. But other traditions also used distinctive bone artifacts. For example, a split-based bone point was made by Aurignacian craftsmen for fairly light spears.

Core and flake tools did not completely disappear during the Upper Paleolithic. Other characteristic tools of the Aurignacian craftsmen included the keel-shaped round scraper and keel-shaped nosed scraper. Both of these implements were made from small cores or rather thick flakes. But the main toolmaking activities during this stage centered on the blade.

The most common blade tool was the chisellike burin, or graver. These implements came in a wide variety of shapes and sizes and were probably used for making grooves or slots. Other artifacts associated with the blade traditions included the notched blade (similar to a spokeshave in function), the awl or drill (used for cutting holes), and various types of projectile points and knives. Some of these can also be distinguished according to tradition. For example, the willow-leaf point was associated with the Solutrean industries, while the backed blade (a knife with one dull side) was most characteristic of the Perigordian.

Eventually replaced around 10,000 years ago, the blade tradition spread throughout most of the Old World—from Siberia to South Africa. Toward the end of the Upper Paleolithic, very tiny blades (microliths) were being manufactured in most of Europe and North Africa. Inserted into the sides of bone or wood projectile points, these microliths represent a new invention which continues into the Mesolithic. As you have noticed, a large variety of Upper Paleolithic traditions existed. Sometimes the term *Aurignacoid* is used to refer to all of them.

EXERCISE: MAKING A STONE TOOL

Early humans could only manufacture implements from the materials provided by nature: wood, skin, bone, teeth, horn, fiber, and stone. Stone has great durability, and some of it can be broken to produce a sharp cutting edge.

DO NOTHING UNTIL YOU HAVE READ THE INSTRUCTIONS. DO NOT BREAK THE ROCKS IN THE CLASSROOM. THEY WILL NEED TO BE TAKEN TO A MORE SUITABLE LOCATION. DO NOT BREAK THE ROCKS WITHOUT FOLLOWING THE SAFETY PRECAUTIONS DESCRIBED.

The type of stone found in any area depends upon the geological history of the region. Most of the land surface of the world is underlain by sedimentary rocks such as shale, limestone, and sandstone. Granite is especially common in many mountainous areas. Lava and basalt are abundant in areas with histories of volcanic activity. The problem is that none of these common rocks are satisfactory for knapping; they merely crumble or shatter into smaller pieces.

The kind of stone which is satisfactory has conchoidal fracture. This means that a blow will detach a shell-like flake. Chert, quartzite, and obsidian were most commonly used for artifacts. Flint is a variety of chert which is particularly strong but brittle. Suitable stones are often found along river beds.

Obsidian is formed by the rapid cooling of lava. It is the most easily worked of any natural substance, and the exercise is written in reference to it. The advantage of obsidian is also its drawback. Broken pieces are extremely sharp. Fracturing it is about the same as breaking a window pane or glass bottle. DO NOT PERFORM THIS EXERCISE IF YOU CANNOT MEET THE SAFETY PRECAUTIONS. Do, however, examine the flakes which have already been detached by other people. The safety precautions are as follows:

1. Wear protective clothing. This means pants, a long-sleeved shirt or sweater, gloves, and eye covering. Prescription lenses, sunglasses, or goggles will serve the purpose.

2. Be careful about the place you select for knapping. It is possible for small slivers of obsidian to flake off, and you do not want them in chairs or carpet. Select a place where all the fragments can be swept away when you finish.

3. Do not strike toward the body. Direct the blows so the flakes will detach in the opposite direction.

4. Do not strike with excessive force. You will have to learn the proper amount of force through experience. The location of the blow is more important than the energy with which you hit it. Light taps are preferable.

Percussion is the simplest method of flaking. The flakes are removed by striking the core. There are several ways to do this. One method is to strike the core against a large anvil stone. Another is to hold a "hammer" in your hand and use it to remove the flakes. The best way to learn is by experiment. You will surely discover that it is not as easy as you thought. The hammer can be another stone. If so, do not pick a soft rock; it will break, and you will observe the consequence with your fingers. We recommend a small wooden mallet.

When the flake comes off, examine the result. In general appearance the core will have a concavity, while the inner surface of the flake has a convex curvature. Near the point of impact on the flake, you should detect a swelling, which is the bulb of percussion. Further down from the bulb of percussion (and radiating in arcs), are the ripple marks. They are concentric rings comparable to the ripples caused by dropping an object into a pool of water. Perpendicular to the ripple marks are more or less straight lines. These are shatter marks and are created by the splitting action of the blow. You may have to detach several flakes to note all of these features. Archaeologists sometimes use them to ascertain whether a stone was flaked by man rather than nature.

The flakes can be put to good purpose. Try using them as a scraper. They will cut wood, and you might use them also to sharpen a stick and produce a spear.

To make a hand axe from the core, detach flakes around both edges. If you prefer, try something else. The drawings in the following figures may give you some ideas.

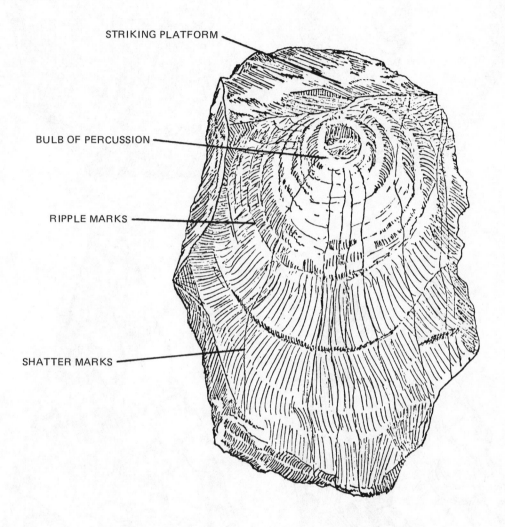

STRIKING PLATFORM

BULB OF PERCUSSION

RIPPLE MARKS

SHATTER MARKS

Figure 4.1. Characteristics of a flake produced by percussion.

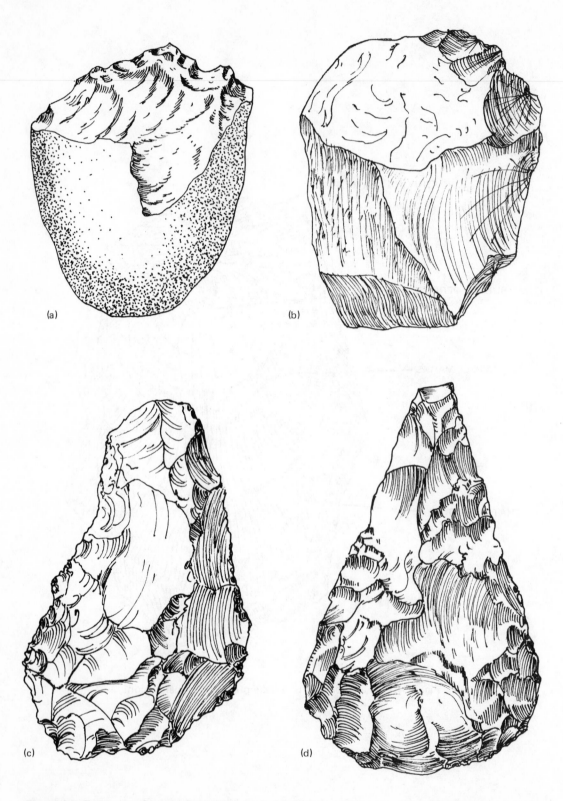

Figure 4.2. Examples of Lower Paleolithic tools. (a) Oldowan pebble tool, (b) Choukoutien chopping tool, (c) Abbevillian hand axe, (d) Acheulean hand axe. Redrawn from Braidwood (1967), Chard (1975), and Clark (1967).

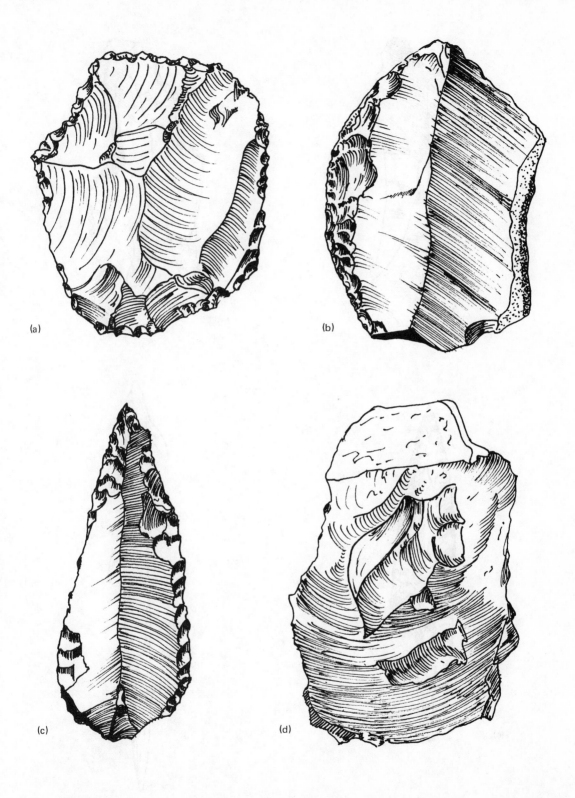

Figure 4.3. Examples of Middle Paleolithic tools. (a) Levalloisian flake, (b) Mousterian side scraper, (c) Mousterian point, (d) Clactonian flake. Redrawn from Brace, Nelson, and Korn (1971), Braidwood (1967), and Movius (1956).

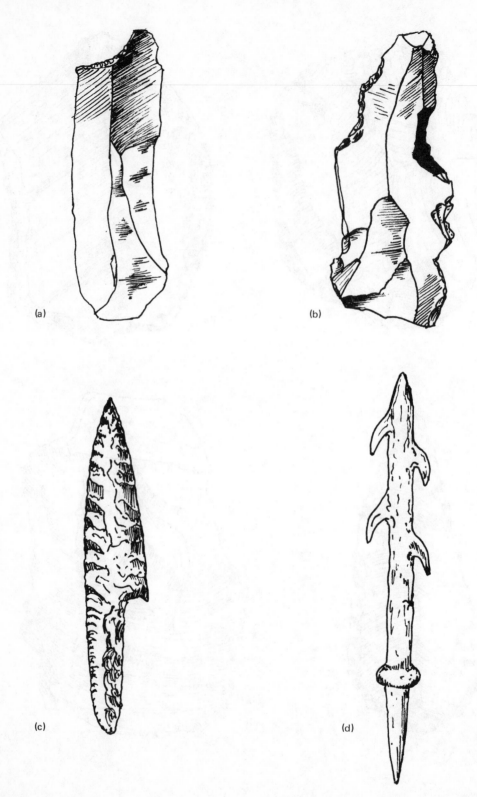

Figure 4.4. Examples of Upper Paleolithic tools. (a) Solutrean burin, (b) Gravettian blade, (c) Solutrean shouldered point, (d) Magdalenian bone harpoon point. Redrawn from Brace, Nelson, and Korn (1971) and Movius (1956).

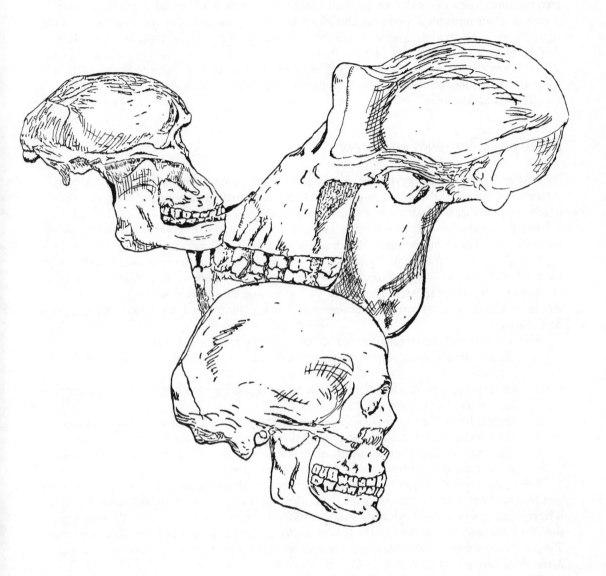

CHAPTER 5

Human Evolution and the Fossil Record

Your professor will probably devote several hours toward describing the fossil evidence for human evolution. This workbook contains some summary and reference material. Some of the major controversies are mentioned. Following this, the remainder of time should be spent on the exercise. If you do the work carefully, you are not likely to finish. Therefore, the casts and skulls should be available at later periods if you need them. We want you to learn enough osteology so that you are able to follow a discussion on the morphology of hominids. There are two parts to the exercise. The first requires learning the names of certain features of the skull. The second part calls for you to identify some specimens.

EVOLUTIONARY TRENDS OF HOMINIDS

Most anthropologists agree that the general evolutionary trends of hominids include three major categories of change. The changes involve locomotion, dental patterns, and mental patterns. It is also widely accepted that our prized superbrains came to us relatively late.

Recall from chapter 1 that the hominid lineage probably began to diverge from the ancestors of the living great apes during the Middle Miocene, about 15 to 18 million years ago.

Several behavioral and anatomical changes were happening. One of the most basic was the attainment of upright posture. No one is certain of the selective forces involved, but probably the carrying of objects (such as food, sticks, and babies) had a lot to do with it. You can see for yourself how difficult it is to carry something while moving on all fours. Try it if you don't think so. What if a lion were chasing you?

The morphological changes associated with bipedalism include the following:
1. The feet became more adapted for support and lost most of their grasping ability in the process.
2. The pelvis became shorter and broader to better support the internal organs and accommodate the altered attachment with the legs.
3. The legs became straighter, longer, and more heavily muscled relative to body weight.
4. The spine acquired a characteristic S-shaped curve to provide a stable center of gravity.
5. The head came to rest more directly on the top of the spine because of the shortening of the jaws and in order to provide a stable center of gravity.

We know these evolutionary trends were happening with about the same certainty you know that you must have had a great-great-great grandfather. The direct evidence of the actual bones, however, is lacking just as it probably is with your relatives so far in the past. It is known that the modifications for bipedalism were present by the time of *Australopithecus,* as early as five million years ago. The postcranial skeleton (everything from the neck down) of *Australopithecus* differs only in slight details from ours.

The teeth, jaws, and palate of early hominids do indicate that our dentition pattern evolved very early. These changes involved:
1. Reduction in the length and size of the canine teeth.
2. Reduction in the length of the snout.
3. Loss of the gaps between the canines and other teeth.
4. More rounding of the dental arcade, so that the jaws came to have a parabolic shape.

Since the time of *Australopithecus,* anatomical changes also occurred with the skull. The most important of these was an increase in the size of the brain. This happened slowly at first; in the last 1 million years, the rate of increase was much more rapid. The cranium itself became more globular. The face and jaws did not protrude as much. The size of the jaws and molar teeth diminished. The head became more rounded. Crests and ridges on the skull generally became less pronounced. The little bony knob behind the bottom of the ear (mastoid process) became larger. The brow ridges over the eyes became less prominent. Much later in time (about 40,000 years ago) the jaws had shrunk so much that a projection on the front (the chin) evolved to provide more strength.

THE PALEONTOLOGICAL RECORD

There are five categories of essential information concerning any taxon of fossils.

1. What is it? This is usually answered by comparison of the morphology. You will therefore need to be acquainted with the osteology of various hominids. This will be described later in the chapter.

2. How old is it? The dating methods, such as mentioned in chapter 2, are applied to the problem. You should not try to memorize the dates of the numerous individual specimens, but do know the time spans for the taxonomic divisions. These will be listed shortly.

3. Where did it live? The most common procedure used to describe this is plotting the geographical distribution of all the known members of the taxon in question. We will do it by listing the major sites. Knowing the names of the sites is also important for another reason— the discoveries are usually named for the location at which they were found.

4. How did it live? This is the question most relevant to our own behavior. However, virtually all the information must rely upon archaeological inference rather than any kind of direct observation.

5. What are its evolutionary relationships? Your goal should be to familiarize yourself with the interpretations concerning the ancestors and descendants. Often, the interpretations of specialists are contradictory. We will mention the major arguments shortly.

Most human paleontologists recognize the following sequence of hominids: (1) *Australopithecus;* (2) *Homo erectus;* (3) Neanderthal; and (4) modern humans. A majority would also agree this temporal sequence is also the pattern of ancestry.

While hundreds of separate *Australopithecus* remains have been found, most of them are fragments. However, the pieces do include virtually all the skeletal parts. The oldest material is at least 5 million years—the youngest about 1 million. Some of the most important sites are included in table 5.1.

TABLE 5.1
Australopithecus Sites

Taung, South Africa	Olduvai, Tanzania
Swartkrans, South Africa	Omo, Ethiopia
Sterkfontein, South Africa	Lothagam, Kenya
Makapansgat, South Africa	Awash, Ethiopia
Kromdraai, South Africa	Lake Rudolf, Kenya

Recent discoveries of *Homo erectus* in Java have extended the age of this species back to 1.9 million B.P. Both the upper and lower time limits have been disputed, mostly over the marginality, with *Homo erectus* compared to early Neanderthals on one hand and to late *Australopithecus* on the other. This is not a surprising circumstance, since evolutionary stages always overlap to some degree. This means you will find different authors giving different dates. We arbitrarily set them between 2 million and 300,000 years B.P.

In contrast to *Australopithecus*, *Homo erectus* is found in both temperate and tropical climates. Some of the most important sites are listed in table 5.2

TABLE 5.2
Homo erectus Sites

Ternifine, Algeria	Choukoutien, China (lower cave)
Olduvai, Tanzania	Lantian, China
Heidelberg, Germany	Trinil, Java (beds)
Vertesszöllös, Hungary	Djetis, Java (beds)

More than fifty places in Europe, Africa, and Asia have produced evidence of *Homo sapiens neanderthalensis*. Some of the best known are found in table 5.3.

TABLE 5.3
Homo sapiens neanderthalensis **Sites**

Swanscombe, England	Shanidar, Iraq
Steinheim, Germany	Mt. Carmel, Israel
Neanderthal, Germany	Broken Hill, Rhodesia
Spy, Belgium	Saldanha, South Africa
La Chapelle, France	Solo, Java
Teshik-Tash, Russia	Mapa, China

Some authorities prefer to place the first two listed specimens (Steinheim and Swanscombe) into *Homo erectus;* others classify them as early Neanderthals. It is a matter of personal taste; they are morphologically intermediate. If they are not included as Neanderthals, the age of the group is from about 100,000 to 35,000 years. If they are, then the age goes back to about 300,000 years. We again arbitrarily take the earlier figure.

Homo sapiens sapiens present distribution is global. The earliest known occurrence of people morphologically indistinguishable from ourselves is at Niah Cave in Borneo, approximately 40,000 years past. By at least 26,000 years ago the modern human had reached Australia. Archaeological evidence suggests that we were present in America perhaps by 35,000 B.P. About the same time span applies to Europe and Africa. We have an antiquity of no more than 50,000 years and an uncertain future.

Our remains are deposited in great numbers across the globe. A few of the most important early locations are cited in table 5.4.

TABLE 5.4
Early *Homo sapiens sapiens* **Sites**

Niah, Borneo	Boskop, South Africa
Lake Mungo, Australia	Cro-Magnon, France
Midland, Texas	Choukoutien, China (upper cave)
Cuzco, Peru	Wadjak, Java

CONTROVERSIES OF HUMAN EVOLUTION

There are two major issues among human paleontologists. The first is: How many kinds of hominids have existed? Secondly, which of them are our direct ancestors?

To speak of "kinds" of organisms is a taxonomic problem, and taxonomists differ in their opinions. They do so for several reasons. First, there is the basic question: What is one kind of organism in the first place?

All the forms of life differ from each other so, in one sense, there are as many different kinds as there are separate entities of existence. The goal of taxonomy is to organize all of this diversity into an order for the convenience of describing and explaining it.

The basic unit of classification is the species. No species is the same as any other, yet all the individuals within it vary among themselves. So how does one decide how and where and when a species starts and stops? It's not easy. Furthermore, there is no universally accepted objective criterion for making a decision.

In theory, a species contains all the members of a closed genetic interchange; that is, members of the same species can all reproduce together and produce offspring of the same kind. Thus those that cannot do so do not belong together. The classic definition states that a species is composed of groups of mutually or potentially interbreeding individuals producing fertile, viable offspring. Crocodiles and crabs do not, so they belong to different species. Beagles and bloodhounds do, so they belong to the same.

The theory is elegant, but its application is not always simple. One problem is that the classic definition can only apply to organisms that reproduce sexually. You can see the problem with *interbreeding* if no interbreeding ever happens. Sex is not necessary; many primitive organisms (such as bacteria) can reproduce asexually.

People, however, do require mates to reproduce. You can't duplicate yourself like a virus or geranium can. The actual or potential interbreeding part of the definition is thus appropriate to humans.

But we are still back at the problem of how to define a species. Some sexually reproducing animals cannot be distinguished by morphological differences, and yet they do not produce fertile, viable offspring when the breeding experiments are tried. Others may be obviously different by human standards, and yet they do interbreed. Sometimes, taxonomists have put them into separate species despite it. Some examples will illustrate the point.

Lions and tigers are readily distinguished. Ordinarily, they do not interbreed, and one of the reasons for this is that they are not usually found together. Taxonomists have traditionally placed them into separate species; the lion is *Panthera leo* and the tiger is *Panthera tigris*. Despite the classification, it is possible to obtain hybrids. They are usually called ligers or tigrons. Coydogs are another case in point. These are the offspring between dogs (*Canis familiaris*) and coyotes (*Canis latrans*).

Sometimes even different genera may hybridize; it is especially common in plants. Catalos, or beefalos, are one illustration among animals; they are crosses between buffalo (*Bison bison*) and cattle (*Bos taurus*).

Extremely closely related species are interreproductively marginal. Crosses between horses and donkeys are good examples. The case is also widely misunderstood. The offspring are not always mules. Neither are mules always male or always sterile.

Producing a mule depends on the sex of the parents. Male and female horses are called *stallions* and *mares* respectively. Male and female donkeys are *jacks* and *jennys*. Mules come only from mares and jacks; they may be either male or female. A stallion crossed with a jenny gives a hinney (which may also be either male or female), which differs from a mule in economic value, strength, appearance, and temperament. The majority of mules are sterile, but a few fertile females have been reported. Some genetic interchange is therefore possible between the two species. Their reproductive isolation is not quite complete even though the difference between horses and donkeys is readily distinguishable to anyone.

Given such problems in defining species among living animals, you can appreciate the difficulty with fossils, in which no breeding experiments are possible. The only recourse is to evaluate similarities in anatomy. But since anatomy does not correlate precisely with reproductive behavior, there must always be doubtful interpretations. The problem is only serious if the organisms are closely related, but this is invariably the case with hominids. Hence, there will always be grounds for argument in trying to separate them into different species.

Yet another problem with the fossil record is that the specimens are fragmentary. Often, they may be single and isolated teeth. This makes the taxonomic assessment more difficult and often leads to highly technical arguments over shreds of evidence which will not resolve the problem anyway. Perhaps an illustration with more familiar circumstances will clarify the point. Suppose you had bones from three skeletons: a dog, a wolf, and a coyote. Could you tell them apart? Not as easily as you might think. All three are so similar and also vary among themselves so that you might make mistakes even with careful study. The errors would multiply if you only had small fragments of the skeleton, such as incisors or tail bones.

Another major difficulty is that all species have a time dimension. *Homo sapiens* for instance is not just the species for living people. It includes all the fossil members of the taxon in the past as well. But the more remotely we go into the past, the less modern our ancestors become. In a continuous process of gradual evolution, where does one draw the line to separate ancestral and descendant groups? It can only be arbitrary.

THE PHYLOGENETIC RELATIONSHIPS OF EARLY HUMANS

As we have stated, there are some fundamental problems of classification which create ambiguity in the interpretation of any group of fossils. The result is that different specialists sometimes have contradictory opinions. This is especially true in human paleontology. You will find that books on the subject use different names for the same known collection of hominids. The ten most commonly used textbooks at the present time present seven different evolutionary schemes. Such contradictory opinions clearly create much confusion for the student. Yet the interpretation of the human record of the past is really what your class is all about. It is better to understand the reasons behind the arguments than to simply learn one or any number of phylogenetic trees. Moreover, new discoveries are continuously being made, and you will better understand their significance by knowing the background behind various interpretations.

Let's take Neanderthals first. By the 1880s, several specimens from Europe were known to scientists. They were all named for the first discovery at Neanderthal in Germany. The fossils appeared to be a rather homogeneous group with surprisingly large brains, but with sloping foreheads, large faces, big brow ridges, and narrow skulls having a sharply angled rear portion of the head. Some scholars believed Neanderthals were too brutal and primitive to be in the direct line of human evolution. It is now known that their primitive features were exaggerated at the time.

The major evidence for Neanderthals not being direct ancestors of modern man came from England. In 1888, a skull and partial skeleton was found at Galley Hill. It had a more modern appearance than Neanderthals but was first thought to be earlier in time—from the early Pleistocene.

Recognize the logic involved. If Galley Hill was more like modern humans than Neanderthals, and if Galley Hill was also older, then Neanderthals were less likely to be our direct ancestors than the population which Galley Hill represented.

The resolution came with subsequent investigations which showed Galley Hill to be a recent burial and not nearly as old as first believed. Thus, the simple explanation for its similarity to modern people is because it is a modern person.

Yet Galley Hill was not the only evidence. Skull and jaw fragments were found at Piltdown, England, in 1912. The braincase was not distinguishable from a modern person's, but the jaw was apelike. Like Galley Hill, the fragments were believed to date from the early Pleistocene. The evidence was widely accepted as genuine, and it implied that the expansion of the brain occurred prior to the acquisition of modern teeth and jaws. Due to the presumed greater antiquity and the modern shape of the Piltdown cranium, the remains were also used to support the idea that Neanderthals were a late, aberrant side branch which became extinct without being directly involved in human evolution.

Again, recognize the logic; a similar situation happens over and over again in the arguments of specialists. The evolution of the head would have been quite confusing if it had had a modern form in the early Pleistocene, a more primitive Neanderthal form later in time, and then suddenly changed again to a modern form. Eliminating the Neanderthals from the lineage would resolve the difficulty.

However, the issue did not need to be resolved, because the problem did not exist. This was finally settled in the 1950s, by which time Piltdown was shown to be a fraud. The head and jaw did not belong together; the latter was the jaw of a modern orangutan, while the braincase belonged to a present-day person. Furthermore, other evidence indicated that a large brain evolved later than changes with the teeth rather than before.

Today there is no good reason for not believing that Neanderthals were our direct ancestors. On the other hand, there is still a controversy about whether some Neanderthal groups were exterminated. Recall that the first discoveries were made in Europe and that they dated from the late Pleistocene, around 100,000 to 35,000 years ago. A few years later, additional specimens were also found in Europe, such as the discoveries in Swanscombe, England, and Fontechevade, France. These remains were fragmentary, but some authorities believed that they were more modern in appearance than the previously known Neanderthals from a later date. Much confusion came from their interpretation.

Added to this came unexpected findings from Palestine. In the years between 1929 and 1934, two caves at Mount Carmel (Skhūl and Tabun) yielded remains in which some individuals were no different from "typical" Neanderthals, while others were more modern.

A theory to explain the observations was fully developed by the first part of the 1950s. This theory recognized two Neanderthal groups: classic and progressive. Modern humans were presumed to have originated from the generally earlier progressive types. This was believed to have happened first in the Near East some 35,000 years ago. Shortly thereafter (as the last glacial stage of Europe passed), their descendants migrated from the Near East into Europe, exterminating the more primitive classic Neanderthals in the process.

This particular theory has now lost much of its influence for several reasons:

1. Newer archaeological work has shown some continuity rather than an abrupt break in the European Middle and Upper Paleolithic traditions. While not conclusive one way or the other, a gradual archaeological transition does not support a sudden replacement by different biological populations. To be sure, the cultural change in Europe at the time is fairly rapid, but it is not so drastic as to require an extinction hypothesis to explain it.

2. Modern humans are now understood to have first occurred prior to 35,000 years ago. Not many, but some. We have already mentioned the date of 40,000 for the Niah population in Borneo. In any event, there is no reason to believe the Near East is the cradle of present humanity.

3. Progressive Neanderthals are more advanced than classic types only in some respects. Such traits do include smaller brow ridges (in most), a more rounded back of the head (in some), and the presence of a chin (in one). None of these really provide substantial evidence that the progressive group was all that progressive. Moreover, the generally later classic type has bigger brains and rounder skulls, both ways in which the progressive variety is actually more primitive.

4. A dichotomy of Neanderthals into two groups fails to accommodate all the individuals known. Specimens from Java and Rhodesia, for example, do not fit well into either type.

Most contemporary interpretations presume that Neanderthals are our immediate ancestors. They varied extensively among themselves, at least as much as or more than people of the present time. There is a tendency to separate them into groups based upon climatic adaptation: glacial, temperate, and tropical. All such divisions, however, are just as arbitrary as racial taxonomies of humans today. Some 30,000 to 40,000 years ago, the human fossil record shows intermediate forms between Neanderthals and modern humans. Some 200,000 to 300,000 years ago, the same situation exists between Neanderthals and *Homo erectus.* This is to be expected with a gradual evolutionary change.

Recognition of *Homo erectus* began in 1891. A Dutch physician, Eugene Dubois, found a skull cap and femur along the Solo River in Java. (With remarkable audacity, he went to Java for the purpose of discovering what he actually did.) The cranial fragment indicated that it belonged to some beetle-browed, small-brained creature, but the leg bone clearly was representative of a fully erect biped. Did they belong together? Dubois assumed they did, and subsequent evidence demonstrated his belief to be correct. The material was originally named *Pithecanthropus erectus,* or erect (walking) ape-person. Closely related forms were later discovered in China and elsewhere. Several were given a variety of names at first, such as *Sinanthropus* and *Atlanthropus.* These are all presently considered to belong to our own genus, *Homo.*

As with Neanderthals and *Australopithecus, Homo erectus* has likewise been claimed to not be our direct ancestor. The reason is now because of a disputed coexistence with another group which some paleontologists recognize as *Homo habilis*. This is an important issue, but let's postpone it until later. In the meantime, *Australopithecus* is another story.

Raymond Dart was a young anatomy professor in South Africa during 1924. In that year, he described an immature hominoid from a site called Taung. The discovery was named *Australopithecus africanus,* or African southern ape. Despite the Greek root for *ape* in the name, Dart argued the individual represented an ancient group of hominids. Many paleontologists did not at first believe his opinion, but they were later convinced when adult individuals of the same taxon were found.

Complications were apparent by 1938; more than a single type appeared. As usual, different generic names were first applied (*Paranthropus, Pleisianthropus,* and so forth). A reaction to this procedure began about a decade later, and the prevailing judgment came to be that they were all members of the early Pleistocene genus with the name which had priority—*Australopithecus.*

This does not necessarily mean they are all the same species. One kind (*A. africanus*) is gracile. Its molar teeth are relatively smaller and more modern. The skull is more globular, and the body size is slight, with a weight of perhaps 80 pounds and a stature of about 4 feet. The second kind (*A. robustus*) is about 5 feet and 120 pounds. Its molars are big and broad. The jaws are massive, and the crests or ridges on the skull more pronounced.

One explanation to account for the difference in teeth is that the dentition reflects a variation in diet; the big ones are thought to be vegetarians, and the small ones to be more carnivorous. The more advanced morphology of the gracile type suggests that the robust forms are only indirectly related to us. Perhaps *A. africanus* and *A. robustus* competed within the same territory, and only *A. africanus* survived.

More complexity came in 1959. Olduvai Gorge in East Africa produced the remains of a hominid even more robust than the bigger South African individuals. The molar teeth were likewise wider. Such differences resulted in naming yet another genus and species—*Zinjanthropus bosei.*

During the 1960s, considerable reaction to the taxonomic jumble had occurred. *Zinjanthropus* was relegated to *Australopithecus.* This left three species at most: *A. robustus, A. bosei,* and *A. africanus.* Most authorities went further, placing the first two in the same species. Whenever this is done, the rules of taxonomy stipulate that the earliest valid name has priority. This means that *A. robustus* is applied to both in correct formality. At last, the interpretations seemed on their way toward less complication and greater agreement.

Even more lumping was also proposed. It was argued that not only are *A. bosei* and *A. robustus* the same species, but so are *A. robustus* and *A. africanus.* You should recall there are differences in size and the ruggedness of the skeleton. Modern men and women vary by a lesser degree by sex for the same characteristics. Great apes have even more of this sexual dimorphism. Perhaps then, the two "species" of *Australopithecus* are actually males and females of the same group.

This is an appealing hypothesis, but there are some problems which it faces. The molar teeth differ by shape as well as size, and this is hard to explain on the basis of sex. The amount of variation in the size of the teeth is also more than sexual dimorphism would justify. It was also claimed the supposed "males" would then have smaller canines than the supposed "females," but this is not known to happen with any primate species. Lastly, the sex ratio should be about 50% of each sex in the various sites, but statistical studies have shown that this is not the case. Nonetheless, the sexual dimorphism issue is still unsettled.

It's time to take stock. When Darwin wrote the *Origin of Species* in 1859, there was virtually no physical evidence that any type of hominid other than modern humans ever existed. A search ensued for our ancestors. By 1924, *Australopithecus, Homo erectus,* and Neanderthals were all documented. It took about sixty years to do it, along with several abortive theories in the process. The next forty years added substantially to the number of examples of each group. The general trend was to make the categories broader. By 1964, the outline of human evolution was reaching a general consensus, with a minor debate still unresolved about the kinds of *Australopithecus.* The partial remains of

Ramapithecus pushed hominids back to some 14 million years ago, but with a lengthy blank space to the early Pleistocene. Since then, the gap has been lessened without the need of new theories. This brings us to the recent renewal of fundamentally different interpretations.

Olduvai Gorge is small by Grand Canyon standards, but it has produced a wealth of human fossils. The Leakey family spent many years with its survey and excavations. Beginning in 1964, Louis Leakey announced discovery of a hominid which was more modern than *Australopithecus* and yet lived at the same time. He called the collection *Homo habilis* and recognized it as distinct mostly on the basis that the brain size was larger than *Australopithecus*. Furthermore, the stratigraphic arrangement suggested that *Homo erectus* should also be removed from our direct ancestry. This returns us to *Homo erectus* where we left them.

You have had an introduction to stratigraphy in chapter 2. Examine Olduvai Gorge in figure 5.1 and draw your own conclusions. Note the implied age relationships between *H. erectus, H. habilis,* and the robust *Australopithecus* specimen (*Zinjanthropus*).

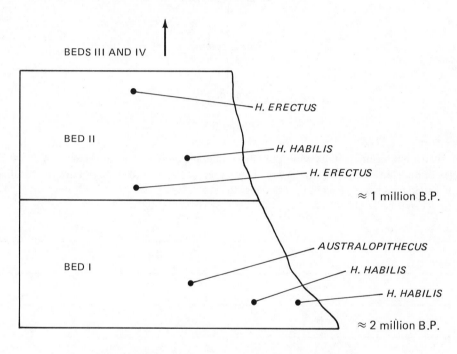

Figure 5.1. Simplified stratigraphy at Olduvai Gorge.

Which of the three groups occurs first? _____

_____

Which of the three groups occurs last? _____

_____

Is *Homo habilis* presumably a contemporary of *Australopithecus* and *Homo erectus?* _____

_____

The implication at the site is that *Homo habilis* does happen earlier than *Australopithecus,* and yet it is a more advanced form. The phylogenetic interpretation is found in figure 5.2.

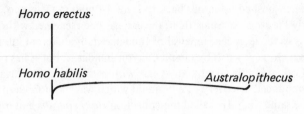

Figure 5.2.

However, also note that *Homo habilis* is found between *Homo erectus* in Bed II. Look at figure 5.3. Would this be their evolutionary relationship?

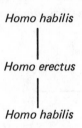

Figure 5.3.

No, such a phylogeny is impossible. Any given lineage could evolve from species A to species B to species C. But this is not the same as A to B and then back again to A. It violates the cardinal definition of a species as having a closed genetic identity.

So how can it be resolved? There are two ways. What are they?

_____

_____

_____

_____

_____

_____

_____

_____

_____

Either the so-called separate species are not actually separate, or the one in the center has to be removed from the lineage. Leakey believed the second choice was correct. Thus, the completed phylogeny is as shown in figure 5.4.

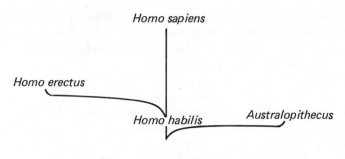

Figure 5.4.

Remember that a phylogeny is not just a way of writing names in a diagram. The arrangement of every single one is a reflection of some particular idea about what happened in the past. For the one above, the theory is that the genus *Homo* has a great antiquity, with *Homo habilis* being the only direct ancestor of *Homo sapiens*. Both *Australopithecus* and *Homo erectus* were closely related to this line but became extinct without leaving more modern descendants.

Immediate and strong reaction to this point of view followed. The point was made that much of the evidence for the existence of *Homo habilis* as a separate taxon was too fragmentary or immature to be diagnostic of any hominid. In addition, the cranial pieces of *"Homo habilis"* (popularly called "Cinderella") which were found in Bed II are what one would expect to find for an early female *Homo erectus*. Finally, it was argued that the *Homo habilis* near the bottom of Bed I could not be distinguished from *Australopithecus africanus*.

Now substitute *Australopithecus* for *Homo habilis* in Bed I and *Homo erectus* for *Homo habilis* in Bed II. The result is figure 5.5.

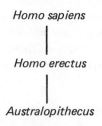

Figure 5.5.

This solution would eliminate the *Homo habilis* problem, since it claims that the species never existed.

But what about the fossils themselves? They can't just be dismissed.

If you follow the second alternative, part of them would belong to one taxon and part of them to another. Suppose you found three skeletons: one of them a complete cow, one a complete horse, and the third being the jumbled remains of both. The mixed remains would be intermediate only because the parts of the two different species were intermixed. The cow-horse combination of bones is not a biologically real animal. Observe how this idea explains why *Homo habilis* would be thought to be more advanced than *Australopithecus;* some of the material includes *Homo erectus*.

Do not think the case is settled. In 1972, Louis Leakey's son, Richard, made a discovery in Kenya which gave added support to the theory of advanced hominids being present at a very early age. Officially, the specimen was designated *Homo species indeterminate,* which means that it was assigned to no particular species in the genus. At the same time, it was believed different from any previously known species. Often, it is referred to by its site number and designation: KNM-ER 1470.

Reconstruction of the shattered braincase indicated a cranial capacity of almost 800 cubic centimeters. For comparison, the average for *A. africanus* is 462. It is 537 for *A. robustus*. If you distinguish *Homo habilis* as valid, the average is 627. Note that the 1470 cranium is considerably more advanced in brain size than any of the three groups.

Some authorities have accepted this as fairly conclusive evidence that *Australopithecus* was not directly related to us. On the other hand, brain size is a characteristic which has much variation among all hominoids. Let's presume for instance that both *Homo habilis* and 1470 do belong to *Australopithecus*. The range in cranial capacity for all its members then varies from 428 to 792 cubic centimeters. This is a proportional difference of 185%. However, *Homo erectus* are already known to vary by 181% and Neanderthals by 174%. Ranges of variation as much as 200% do occur among living people, but this is not common. At any rate, the value for *Australopithecus* is not extraordinary even with hominid 1470 included within it.

And so the issues continue. We started with the question: How many kinds of hominids existed? And, what are their evolutionary relationships? The conclusion is that the matter is still unsettled. Moreover, in concentrating upon the nature of the debate, we have sometimes oversimplified the specific arguments. What you probably want is a simple answer, but the problem is that there is no consensus. At least 10 different phylogenetic interpretations have been advocated by various authorities.

Our own is highly conservative. We believe humans evolved from *Australopithecus, Homo erectus,* and Neanderthals to modern people in a direct and gradual progression. We further believe that only one species of hominid existed at any given time. In our view, early hominids are too closely related to be conclusively distinguished as separate contemporary species. We regard the widely divergent classifications as circumstantial evidence for the point. The coexisting "species" of others are thus taken as ecotypes (subspecific varieties).

However, there are more differences between these ecotypes than presently exist between groups of living humans. We think in part that there are cultural reasons for this; populations which are culturally more primitive have greater amounts of biological heterogeneity between them. The basis for this statement is found in chapter 9. For the moment, we must add that this is a new way of interpreting biological traits and that it has not been widely tested. Finally, many paleontologists regard the single species hypothesis as being too radical and too simple.

EXERCISE: COMPARING FOSSIL SPECIMENS

A. Terminology

Since class time is limited, and some of it will be required for part B, it is important that you carefully study as much as possible beforehand. Specimens are often identified by comparison to a diagnosis, or a formal description of the characters of a particular taxon. We are going to give you some diagnoses. They are not simplified, and are representative of the kind of descriptions which anthropologists use in practice. They are almost taken verbatim from Le Gros Clark (1964).[1] Start by scanning them just for an overall idea.

Australopithecus: *A genus of the Hominidae distinguished by the following characters: relatively small cranial capacity, ranging from about 450 to well over 600 cc.; strongly built supra-orbital ridges; a tendency in individuals of larger varieties for the formation of a low sagittal crest in the frontoparietal region of the vertex of the skull (but not associated with a high nuchal crest); occipital condyles well behind the mid-point of the cranial length but on a transverse level with the auditory apertures; nuchal area of occiput restricted, as in* Homo; *consistent development (in immature as well as mature*

[1] Reprinted from *The Fossil Evidence for Human Evolution* (1964, 2nd ed.) by W. E. LeGros Clark by permission of The University of Chicago Press. ©1964 by The University of Chicago. All rights reserved.

skulls) of a pyramidal mastoid process of typical hominid form and relationships; mandibular fossa constructed on the hominid pattern but in some individuals showing a pronounced development of the postglenoid process; massive jaws, showing considerable individual variation in respect of absolute size; mental eminence absent or slightly indicated; symphysial surface relatively straight and approaching the vertical; dental arcade parabolic in form with no diastema; spatulate canines wearing down flat from the tip only; relatively large premolars and molars; anterior lower premolar bicuspid with subequal cusps, pronounced molarization of first deciduous molar; progressive increase in size of permanent lower molars from first to third; the limb skeleton (so far as it is known) conforming in its main features to the hominid type but differing from Homo *in a number of details, such as the forward prolongation of the region of the anterior superior spine of the ilium and a relatively small sacroiliac surface, the relatively low position (in some individuals) of the ischial tuberosity, and the marked forward prolongation of the intercondylar notch of the femur.*

Homo erectus: *A species of the genus* Homo *characterized by a cranial capacity of about 1,000 cc.; marked platycephaly, with little frontal convexity; massive supra-orbital tori; pronounced post-orbital constriction; opisthocranion coincident with the inion; vertex of skull marked by sagittal ridge; mastoid process variable, but usually small; thick cranial wall; tympanic plate thickened and tending toward a horizontal disposition; broad, flat nasal bones; heavily constructed mandible, lacking a mental eminence; teeth large, with well developed basal cingulum; canines sometimes projecting and slightly interlocking, with small diastema in upper dentition; first lower premolar bicuspid with subequal cusps; molars with well differentiated cusps complicated by secondary wrinkling of the enamel; second upper molar may be larger than the first, and the third lower molar may exceed the second in length; limb bones not distinguishable from those of* H. sapiens.

Homo [sapiens] neanderthalensis: *The skull is distinguished by an exaggerated development of a massive supra-orbital torus, forming an uninterrupted shelf of bone overhanging the orbits (with complete fusion of the ciliary and orbital elements); absence of a vertical forehead; marked flattening of the cranial vault (platycephaly); relatively high position of the external occipital protuberance and the development (usually) of a strong occipital torus; a massive development of the naso-maxillary region of the facial skeleton, with an inflated appearance of the maxillary wall; a heavy mandible, lacking a chin eminence; a pronounced tendency of the molar teeth to taurodontism (that is, enlargement of the pulp cavity with fusion of the roots); a relatively wide sphenoidal angle of the cranial base (about 130°); angular contour of the occiput; certain morphological details of the ear region of the skull (including the rounded or transversely elliptical shape of the auditory aperture, the conformation of the mastoid process, and of the mandibular fossa); a slightly backward disposition of the foramen magnum; and a large cranial capacity (1,300-1,600 cc.). The limb skeleton is characterized by the coarse build of the long bones (which show pronounced curvatures and relatively large extremities), the morphological features of the pubic bone, and by certain morphological details of the talus and calcaneus bones of the ankle, which are said to be somewhat "simian" in character. In addition, the vertebrae of the cervical region of the spine in some cases show a striking development of the spinous processes, which, however, though somewhat simian in appearance, does not exceed the extreme limits of variation in* H. sapiens.

Homo sapiens sapiens: *A [sub] species of the genus* Homo *characterized by a mean cranial capacity of about 1,350 cc.; muscular ridges on the cranium not strongly marked; a rounded and approximately vertical forehead; supra-orbital ridges usually moderately developed and in any case not forming a continuous and uninterrupted torus; rounded occipital region with a nuchal area of relatively small extent; foramen magnum facing directly downward; the consistent presence of a prominent mastoid process of pyramidal shape (in juveniles as well as adults), associated with a well-marked digastric fossa and occipital groove; maximum width of the calvaria usually in the parietal region and axis of glabello-maximal length well above the level of the external occipital protuberance; marked flexion of the sphenoidal angle, with a mean value of about 110°; jaws and teeth of relatively small size, with retrogressive features in the last molars; maxilla having a concave facial surface, including a canine fossa; distinct mental eminence; eruption of permanent canine commonly preceding that of the second molar; spines of cervical vertebrae (with the exception of the seventh) usually rudimentary; appendicular skeleton adapted for a fully upright posture and gait; limb bones relatively slender and straight.*

Almost certainly, there were so many unfamiliar words in the diagnoses that you had difficulty in understanding them.

Let's solve this problem with a short anatomy lesson.

Each of the technical terms will be defined as simply as possible. All of the features should be located on the modern human skulls available in the classroom. We have also included some labeled pictures for reference. However, you should not rely excessively upon the drawings since the three-dimensional real skulls show the labeled features more clearly.

We do not expect you to bother with any of the minor differences for any skeletal parts other than the skull. The italicized words in the lesson refer to the same words as mentioned in the diagnoses.

Stop! You are not yet ready to pick up anything.

Skulls are fragile, especially many of the archaeological specimens. Do not lift them by poking fingers into the eye sockets or by any other projection, loop, or "handle." Grasp the top of the skull about halfway between the front and back. After you lift it, cradle it in both hands. You have in your hands what was once a living person. It is unconscionably thoughtless to damage the remains through negligence or flippancy.

To find your way around the bones, you need directions. All of these refer to the head in its normal position (sitting on top of the neck). *Anterior* is forward (toward the tip of the nose). *Posterior* is backward. *Superior* is on top; *inferior* on the bottom. *Lateral* means on the sides, as the ears are.

Turn the skull and look at the bottom (*inferior portion*). Turn the teeth away from you and see the big hole (*foramen magnum*). It is the entrance to the head through which the spinal cord passes. On the lateral and anterior surfaces of the foramen magnum, note the two rounded bumps called the *occipital condyles.* Keep going in a lateral direction until you come to the breast-shaped *mastoid processes.* Observe there is one on each side. No, they are not the sharp, narrow spines which you may see nearby, but the gently rounded ones in back of and down from the ear holes.

Move your eyes and fingers all the way to the most posterior and inferior portion of the skull. This is the *external occipital protuberance.* Feel for it on the back of your own head. Look between this bump and the foramen magnum. The general area is the *nuchal region.* You should be able to see one or more crescent-shaped ridges arching in the back of the foramen magnum. If the most prominent ridge is very strongly developed, it is called the *nuchal crest.* In modern humans, there are less prominent *nuchal lines* instead. Whenever a line or sharp ridge is prominent, it is a crest.

Now move to the top of the skull. Looking straight down upon it, observe the seamlines between the bones (*sutures*). Note the T-shaped intersection (*bregma*) on the very top. This is a marked "soft spot" (*fontanelle*) on a baby.

Notice that one suture on the top is crosswise (*transverse*). Another runs lengthwise in the same direction as the nose and back of the neck. It is the *sagittal suture,* and it stops at the bregma, which separates the big, single frontal bone from the big, flatter *parietal* bones on the sides. Look at the area where the sagittal suture lies. If there is a strongly developed ridge, it is a *sagittal crest.* In modern humans, you will not see a crest, but you may find a slight elevation.

Again move laterally to the sagittal suture, and see how the parietal bones form a large, gently curved region occupying most of the side of the head. This is the *parietal region.* The *fronto-parietal region* is appropriately just in front of it—to the side and back of the forehead.

Next, rotate the skull so that the eye sockets (*orbits*) are staring at you. You will probably find a slight ridge slightly above and between the orbits. These are the *supra-orbital* or *brow ridges.* Lateral and posterior to the brow ridges is the *post-orbital constriction*. It is an inward curvature of the skull on both sides.

Pick up the lower jaw (the *mandible*). The upper jaw is the *maxilla*. Both of them contain teeth. The upper and lower jaws have 32 teeth if all of them are present. Many of the teeth on your specimen will probably be missing, but there should be enough of them left to see that there are four kinds. The *molars* are all the way to the back. They will have several small bumps on the top (*cusps*). The *premolars* (dentists call them *bicuspids*) are *bicuspid* (they have two cusps). The *canines* have a single point. The *incisors* are all the way to the front. They also have a single edge, and are spadelike or *spatulate* in appearance.

You will probably not find any gaps between the teeth except for the holes which obviously represent teeth which have fallen out. If you do find a gap, it is a *diastema*. More than one of them are called *diastemata*. At the front of the mandible is the *mental eminence* or chin.

The skull (*cranium*) is the whole head including the mandible. Removing the mandible leaves you with the *calvarium*. If you further removed the facial region (please don't try) only the braincase would be left.

The *opisthocranion* is a point used as a landmark. It is the most posterior point of the skull not including the external *occipital protuberance*. The *inion* is another landmark and is located at the furthest point of the external occipital protuberance.

This short lesson has told you where to find most of the features that Le Gros Clark used to distinguish the different taxa of fossil hominids. Remember that they were examples of how paleontologists talk to each other. They should now make sense. After you locate the features on a modern human, review the diagnoses, looking at your specimen as you read them again.

Memorizing names is pretty dull, but you need them for part B. Do it as soon as possible.

B. Comparing Specimens

Several hundred specimens of hominids having great antiquity have been discovered. More are continually being found. Each needs to be identified. This is usually done by comparison of characters. Almost always, such a comparison reveals that the specimen belongs to a species which is already known, and it becomes another example.

For this exercise, we want you to compare some "unknown" specimens to casts and skulls representing the four groups described in the four diagnoses. On the basis of this comparison, you should be able to decide to which group it belongs. You may decide that it does not fit any of them. We don't care, but we do want you to give some justification for whatever your conclusion is. We think that it is better to learn by practice than by merely being told. Bear in mind though, that the exercise is artificial, and that taxonomy is not as casual as one might gather from the assignment.

First, scrutinize the examples. The casts represent *Australopithecus, Homo erectus, H. sapiens neanderthalensis,* and *H. sapiens sapiens*.

There are two examples of *Australopithecus*. One came from Sterkfontein in South Africa and is popularly called Mrs. Ples. It is thought to be a female and, therefore, is less rugged than the skull of a male would be. From this you should gather that differences between sexes have to be borne in mind whenever one is classifying fossils.

The second example comes from Swartkrans, South Africa. Notice that the skull is rather badly crushed; this will be another complication in your comparison. The Swartkrans cast is representative of the robust *Australopithecus* type. Notice the sagittal crest. This is for the attachment of powerful jaw muscles, and suggests that the individual was a male.

Homo erectus is represented by material from Choukoutien in Northern China. The population is more modern in appearance than most *Homo erectus* forms. They are not as old as most *Homo erectus* discoveries have been. The age is probably not more than 400,000 years; some *H. erectus* finds from Java are almost 2 million years old.

There are a variety of Neanderthals for comparison. If you are interested in their particular names, the instructor can identify them.

You also have some modern human skulls, both archaeological and quite recent. They have been selected to give you an idea of the normal range of variation.

The best way to start the exercise is by reminding yourself that all individuals vary. Do not, therefore, presume that some unknown specimen must be exactly like the sample in order to belong to the same taxon. Briefly examine several of the modern skulls. *At the absolute minimum* you should find more variation than you see here before concluding any two of the cases in the exercise belong to separate species.

Now compare some of the unknown material to the reference and diagnoses. Try to decide for yourself what it is.

In this assortment are bones and broken pieces of casts. Some pieces may not even be hominid, and there are a few that are meant to be confusing. Note that much of it is fragmentary.

Excellent—this is exactly the way most fossils are. In the next meeting, the instructor will identify the material according to the number taped on it. Try to do as many as you can—at least two.

Case number:_____

I think this is_____ for the following reasons:

_____

_____

_____

_____

_____

Case number: _____

I think this is_____ for the following reasons:

_____

_____

_____

_____

_____

_____

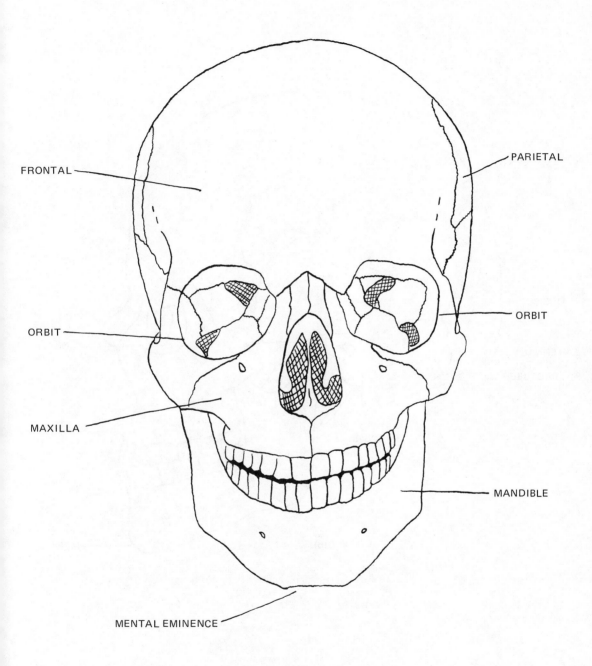

FRONTAL

PARIETAL

ORBIT

ORBIT

MAXILLA

MANDIBLE

MENTAL EMINENCE

Figure 5.6. Anterior view of modern skull.

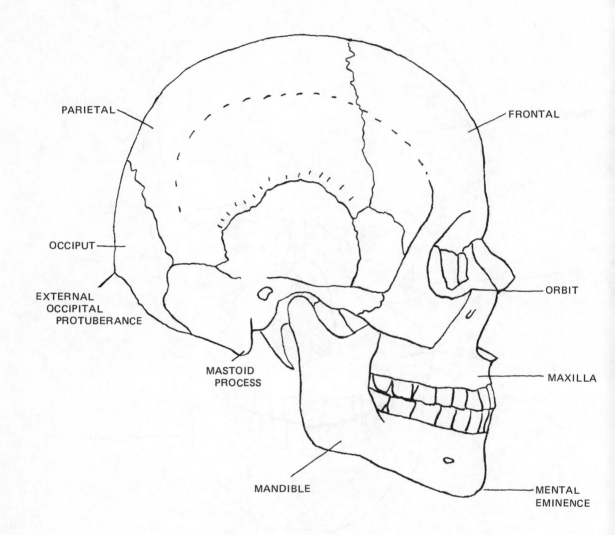

Figure 5.7. Lateral view of modern skull.

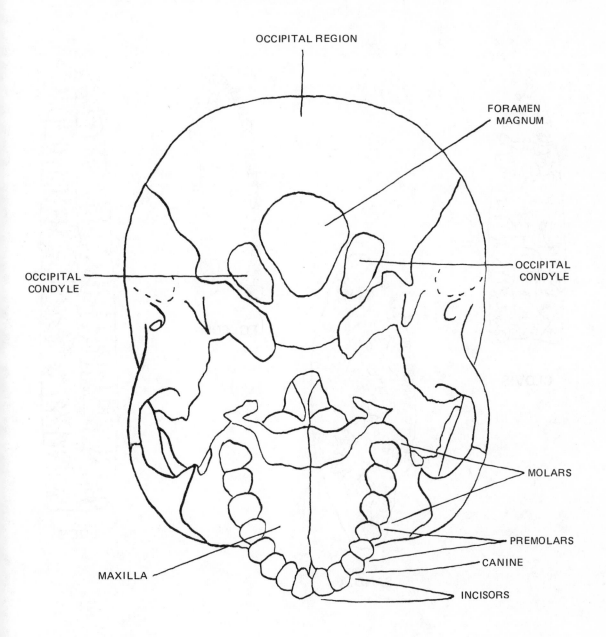

Figure 5.8. Inferior view of modern skull.

CLOVIS

SANDIA

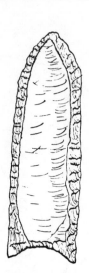

FOLSOM

EDEN

CHAPTER 6
North American Prehistory

Chapter 6 has several goals. First, we want to mention the developmental sequence commonly used in American archaeology. It will be compared to the corresponding series of stages in the Old World. Some illustrations will be given for each of the major periods. An exercise on seriation is included to show how sites or artifacts can be placed in chronological order through the comparison of several locations.

NEW WORLD CULTURAL EVOLUTION

If everyone used the same words to describe the archaeological record everywhere in the world it certainly would be convenient, but unfortunately, this is not the case. Therefore, you need to learn a separate list which applies to North and South America. Even though the names are different for the Old and New Worlds, some comparable basic life-styles did exist. Refer to table 6.1 to see how they correspond.

Next, examine table 6.2. It provides dates and examples of North American stages. Many more examples could be given; we have only given those specifically mentioned in the text. The Classic and Postclassic periods apply only to those portions of the New World having civilizations. These will be described in chapter 7.

No part of native America north of central Mexico developed a civilization in the anthropological meaning, which implies the presence of densely populated urban centers. Most of the Indians of the United States were living at a Formative level when first encountered by Europeans. This refers to a farming and village life-style similar to the Neolithic of the Old World. The remainder were hunters and gatherers living a life-style which also existed in the Archaic. In other words, more than a single evolutionary stage existed at the same time.

Confusing? Yes, but the culture of any people depends not only upon the time at which they live, but also upon where they live. You, for instance, are a member of an industrial state. So are the numerical majority of the rest of the world's people. Yet even today, it is possible to find some human groups with the technology and social organization typical of a much earlier time. An extreme example are the Tasaday from a remote part of the Philippines. This very small society was only discovered a few years ago, and their artifacts and social organization are about the same as one could expect to find a million years past.

Such a great difference as that between people of the Space Age and those of the Stone Age is not ordinary, but the point is to recognize how common it is for different stages of evolution to be partially contemporaneous. The dates given to them are usually selected according to the time when the stage first happened someplace.

A short way to make this point is by stating that some people have more primitive lives than others. *Primitive* in evolutionary theory means one thing only: "more like the ancestral form." This is not the same as "earlier in time," "more natural," "less disturbed," "apelike," "ignorant," "backward," or "simple."

For example, the hands of a person are more primitive than the hooves of a horse. The ancestors of mammals (including both horses and people) had hands and feet with five digits. Our hands have not changed as much from this pattern as have horses' hooves. For them, there is only one functional digit despite the fact that their ancestors had five. So, a horse's hoof is less primitive or more advanced because it has changed more from the ancestral condition. And, to repeat, it is not because humans are earlier, more natural, less disturbed, or more ignorant, backward, or simple than horses.

The same circumstance applies to societies and to parts of societies. Whatever it is, something is more primitive only if it resembles the ancestral state more closely. There is but one important qualification. Our knowledge of the ancestral state can change. If it does, our opinion about what is or is not primitive may also change.

The illustrations on the preceding page were redrawn from Jennings (1974).

TABLE 6.1
Comparison of Old and New World Stages of Cultural Evolution

SUBSISTENCE	NEW WORLD	OLD WORLD
Agricultural	Postclassic	Civilization
	Classic	
	Formative	Neolithic
Preagricultural	Archaic	Mesolithic
	Lithic	Upper Paleolithic
	None	Middle Paleolithic
		Lower Paleolithic

TABLE 6.2
Stages, Examples, and Dates Before the Present for American Archaeology

STAGE	DATE B.P.	EXAMPLES
Postclassic	1050 to 450	Toltec, Aztec
Classic	1650 to 1050	Teotihuacan, Maya
Formative	3500 to 1650	Woodland tradition
Archaic	8000 to 3500	Cascade phase
Upper Lithic	14,000 to 8000	Big Game tradition
Lower Lithic	35,000? to 14,000	Scattered sites only

Lithic

Virtually all anthropologists agree that the ancestors of the Native Americans migrated from Siberia. Asia and North America were conjoined several times in the past in the region of the Bering Strait, and the area (including what was once dry land) is known as Berengia. This connection is usually called a land bridge; the so-called bridge was sometimes a vast area about a thousand miles wide.

The number of migrants crossing to North America must have been small. How small? No one knows, but at most there may have been a few hundred individuals during the entire time the continents were still connected.

We can only call them *migrants* today. They probably did not realize they were leaving one continent and entering another. Anyone moving between Alaska and Siberia at that time would find themselves on a flat plain which stretched for hundreds of miles. Gradually following the wandering herds of animals, their descendants eventually became dispersed throughout the Americas.

We have almost no direct knowledge about the earliest migrants. You should be able to see why this is so. Imagine the population of your college dispersed into small bands over the 16 million square miles of two continents. Then take away virtually all of their material possessions, wait for 30,000 years, and try to find some trace of the original groups. A formidable task indeed.

Despite this difficulty, evidence for the early occupation of America is increasing continuously. For example, a bone flesher from the Old Crow site in the Yukon has recently been radiocarbon dated at 27,000 B.P.

What did these people look like? Direct skeletal evidence is very sparse. Moreover, some of it is not reliably dated. This is the case with the human bones found at Lagoa Santa, Brazil; Cuzco, Peru; and Punin, Ecuador. These probably have an age greater than 10,000 years, but uncertainty exists. One skull portion from Laguna Beach, California has been radiocarbon dated at 17,000 years. A skull from Midland, Texas may be about 18,000 years. The oldest remains from the northwestern United States have been found in southeastern Washington at the Marmes Rock Shelter. They have an age of about 11,000 years.

This says something about where the remains of early humans in America come from and how old they are, but nothing about the question we asked concerning what they looked like. Well, the answer is not very satisfactory anyway. A skeleton provides only limited clues toward the external appearance of an individual. Features such as the color of the skin, the amount and distribution of the hair, and the shape of the nose can only be intelligently guessed. As far as we know, the small number of bones tells us that Lower Lithic people were not very different from present-day American Indians. Furthermore, we should not expect much difference; 30,000 years is only an eye blink in evolutionary time. No evidence of Neanderthals (or any earlier stage) has ever been discovered on our two continents, and there is no strong reason to believe it will ever be.

Archaeologists divide the Lithic into two parts: the Lower and the Upper. As with the biological evidence, the cultural circumstances of the first part are strongly inferential. Pieces of worked bone, fire hearths, and crude flakes of stone provide nearly all the direct information. No one has yet identified a projectile point with such antiquity. In fact, the Lower Lithic has also been named the Preprojectile Point Horizon.

Since everyone believes that these people were hunters and gatherers and hence were surely killing animals, the question becomes why there are no projectile points.

What kind of hypotheses suggest themselves to you? Compare your thoughts on the subject to the list at the end of the chapter.

In contrast to the Lower portion, the Upper Lithic is well documented. It began about 14,000 years ago and is divided into three traditions: Paleoeastern, Paleowestern, and Paleonorthern. The northern tradition occupied arctic regions and is not as old as the others. The Paleoeastern is somewhat deceptively named, since it extended as far west as the Rocky Mountains. The western adaptation extended from the Rockies to the Pacific coast.

This scheme is not quite so simple. The Paleoeastern for example has two names. It is also called the Big Game Hunting tradition. As the name implies, it is identified with a specialization in the killing of large animals. It is both a romantic and dramatic stereotype.

Some 15,000 years ago, the Great Plains of North America contained a fauna which is only weakly paralleled by the African savannah at present. Gigantic species of extinct bison, mammoths, mastodons, horses, camels, and glyptodons were all preyed upon by early Indians. It must have been a hunter's paradise. Some anthropologists believe the hunters were so adept that they were a major factor in causing the extinction of the animals they depended upon. As you might expect, projectile points were important. They were attached to spears, not arrows, for the bow and arrow had not yet been invented.

At this point we want to interject some thoughts. Projectile points are analogous to guns in our own society; everyone knows about them and many individuals own them. They are still, however, only a small portion of our total inventory of material items. Like the metal of a rifle, the points are made from hard substances which will be preserved for a long time. Thus, they will be archaeologically represented in a greater proportion than items having less permanence. Archaeologists do not have some bizarre affection for arrowheads or spear points. If you've seen one, you've seen them all. Nonetheless, they may provide the bulk of knowledge about a particular period of time. It should also be recognized that a particular type of point has no necessary connection with a particular group of people. One population might manufacture several types of points, and a single type may be made by several groups.

The people of the Big Game tradition made some points which are diagnostic. Examples include the Sandia, Clovis, Folsom, and Eden. All of these require great skill in their manufacture. Eden points are parallel-flaked blades done with such aesthetic precision that they are among the finest examples of stone tools anywhere in the world.

Archaic

The life-style of the Archaic stage throughout North America was based upon a less spectacular pattern of subsistence. It was not fundamentally different from the preceding Upper Lithic in the western portion of the United States.

Around 9000 years ago, mastodons, mammoths, glyptodons, and horses were on their way to extinction. Much later, horses would be reintroduced by Europeans. The archaic species of giant bison also disappeared, but the smaller modern buffalo (*Bison bison*) managed to survive.

With such a change in the fauna and also with a warmer and dryer climate, the descendants of the Big Game hunters gradually shifted their economy toward more diversification. Smaller animals continued to be hunted, but a greater emphasis appears to have been placed on the gathering of plants.

We want to make a general point about such hunting and gathering societies. Only in unusual circumstances (such as with the recent Eskimo) does hunting provide most of the food supply. Berry picking, root digging, and insect grabbing are more reliable. This is women's work, and women provide most of the food even in so-called hunting societies. It is the everyday, ordinary collection that gives security.

Archaic groups existed with considerable regional variation. However, all of them lacked agriculture. This distinguishes them from the Formative. To separate them from the Upper Lithic, a number of traits have been suggested. These include the bow, dog burials, and polished stone tools. Nonetheless, these traits are not found in all Archaic sites.

Toward the end of this stage, some experiments with domestication were taking place. The earliest cases may have been with sunflowers and Jerusalem artichokes. Other plants were also gradually being cultivated. A list of foods still important to us today includes squash, gourds, chili peppers, avocados, pumpkins, beans, potatoes, tomatoes, tobacco, and corn. All of these were originally cultivated by the South or North American Archaic peoples. Their everyday, ordinary collections now provide us with a large part of the food and drugs for our own everyday, ordinary survival.

Formative

If you have been to the Midwestern part of the United States, you have surely heard about the "Mound Builders." Before the advent of modern archaeology, they were thought to be a mysterious race of extinct people (perhaps from Israel or Atlantis) who constructed large mounds of earth after somehow migrating to America. Whites found it hard to believe that the ancestors of the Indians living in the same region were capable of building such massive earthworks. Yet they were, and they did. We have selected them to illustrate the Formative stage. Within this stage, the examples belong to the Woodland and Mississippian traditions.

The Adena complex is representative of early Woodland. Adena sites are located in southern Ohio, southeastern Indiana, northern Kentucky, southwestern Pennsylvania, and northwestern West Virginia. See the map (figure 6.1).

The people lived in fairly large circular houses, two to five of them making a small village. A dispersed community organization was formed by linkages (probably based on kinship ties) between

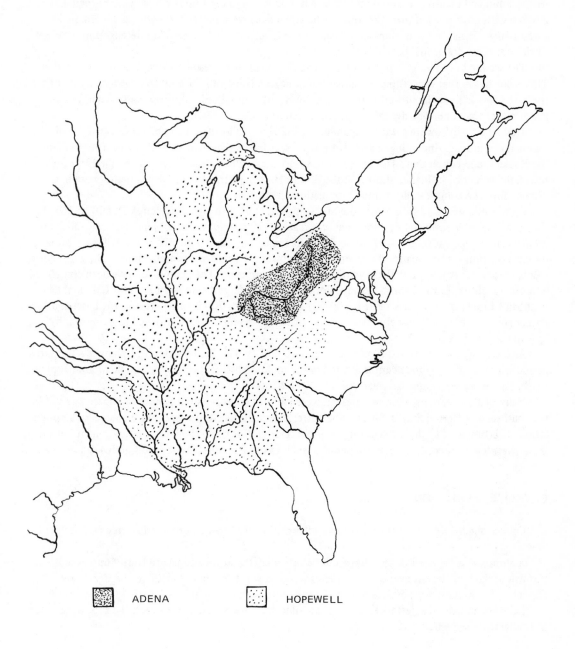

Figure 6.1. Distribution of Adena and Hopewell. Redrawn from Jennings (1974).

several of the local settlements. This larger aggregation or "greater village" provided enough individuals to build and maintain a burial mound. Such mounds were log tombs which were burned and covered with great piles of dirt. Commonly the larger sites were associated with earthwork enclosures. Being circular in form, they are considered to be ceremonial rather than defensive in function. Such locations were probably political and religious centers.

The second burial mound phase is known as Hopewell. It represents a continuation of the first. This is not to say that everything remained the same, for Hopewell differed from Adena by distinctive traits and artifacts identified with the mortuary cult. Burial mounds were constructed in two stages rather than one. The design and types of materials also differed.

Trading networks were greatly expanded during Hopewell times. The objective was to obtain exotic raw materials—including copper from the Great Lakes, obsidian and grizzly bear teeth from the Rockies, and conch shells from the southeastern coast. During the latter part of the Hopewell phase, the center of influence shifted to the South. Here, new traits from Mesoamerica were incorporated into the complex and created a transitional period.

From this a new tradition arose: the Mississippian. During this time (about A.D. 500 to 1650), the apex for eastern cultural development was reached. Heavier population densities occurred. Ceremonial centers became larger, with some residents remaining throughout the year. Although burial mounds continued to be made, they were overshadowed by the larger temple mounds. Labor requirements for the construction of these artificial hills were immense. They could not have been completed without a highly organized social system. For example, the largest temple mound (at Cahokia, near East Saint Louis) is truly massive. It is 100 feet high, measures 700 by 1000 feet at the base, and covers 16 acres. Before it was completed, nearly 22 million cubic feet of dirt had to be moved by human hand and backs.

Archaeologists break the Mississippian into two phases. The Temple Mound I phase is a formative period with its most vigorous center located in the middle Mississippi Valley. Temple Mound II phase reached a climax in Georgia between A.D. 1200 and 1500.

Many of these centers, such as Cahokia, were still in existence when Spanish explorers arrived in the southeastern United States. Shortly thereafter, the introduced diseases created a decline in population. This brings us to the ethnographic present. During this time, the line of development between the archaeological record and historic peoples (such as the Iroquois, Creek, and Caddo) can be traced.

EXERCISE: SERIATION

Comparing different sites provides more information than can be obtained from examining only one.

Assume we knew the stratigraphic sequence at six different locations, arbitrarily numbered 1 through 6. Each of the sites varied from the others, but some overlap of artifacts did occur. By matching the overlap, it is possible to correlate the different stratigraphies together.

Let's use alphabetical letters to represent artifacts. At the six sites, we found the following types in stratigraphic sequence.

			Sites		
1	2	3	4	5	6
O	T	R	R	B	M
R	S	B	Y	T	O
B	Y	T	C	S	R

Some of the chronological associations may be seen at a glance. At site 5, for instance, artifact type S is older than T, and T is older than B. Others are not so obvious. How, for example, does site 6 compare to 5? None of the artifacts are the same. Despite this, one could establish the relationship between all of the sites by placing everything in its proper order.

The first step is to find some kind of match anywhere. It doesn't matter what you select at the beginning. Let's try it.

Notice that B is found in site 3 as well as site 1. Match the B's as follows.

1	3
O	
R	R
B	B
	T

We now know that artifact T is older than O even though they were not found at the same location. So far, the extended sequence is T–B–R–O.

Next, continue with the matching process until all the artifacts are relatively dated. The final result is:

1	2	3	4	5	6
					M
O					O
R		R	R		R
B		B		B	
	T	T		T	
	S			S	
	Y		Y		
			C		

This process is called *seriation*. It permitted us to establish the entire series in chronological order. Merely read from bottom to top: C–Y–S–T–B–R–O–M. Further, note that site 4 represents the earliest occupation and that site 6 represents the youngest. Note the big gap in the series at site 4. Perhaps the place was abandoned for a period of time and then later reoccupied.

Thus, in addition to extending a chronology, seriation may provide some insight into the region's cultural history. The method can be used for other types of data. A paleontologist could do the same with different kinds of species found at different places. It is a fundamental and simple way of discovering more about the past.

Try it for yourself on the following problem.

		Sites		
1	2	3	4	5
P	V	K	Z	P
L	Z	L	I	K
A	M	A	M	U

Is the seriation of some of the objects uncertain? What information is needed to complete it?

_____

_____

_____

Answer to problem on page 71:

Why are there no projectile points in the Lower Lithic? Since the answer to this problem is unknown, there is obviously no correct answer. Some hypotheses are the following:

1. Perhaps the problem does not exist. In other words, the evidence for humans being in America prior to 15,000 B.P. may be incorrectly interpreted. This implies an elegant solution; there were no people around to make the points in the first place.
2. They were being made, but the number of individuals was so small and the particular artifacts so rare that the odds of discovering one of them are very low.
3. The points have already been discovered, but not recognized for what they are. Perhaps, for instance, the points were composite microliths—a series of very tiny flakes attached to the end of a spear. After the wooden portion of the implement has decayed, the tiny flakes at the end would be difficult to recognize for their true significance. Only the most painstaking excavation technique could provide the evidence.
4. Finally, the most obvious hypothesis is that the lack of evidence means what it appears to mean—points just weren't being produced. Remember that gathering is ordinarily more important than hunting, and even if hunting is done with high frequency, there are still ways to kill animals without spear points. Using traps and weirs is one way to catch them. Driving game over cliffs is another common technique. Clubs and sharpened sticks can be used to dispatch the prey, especially if it can be immobilized beforehand.

It doesn't matter if your hypotheses were different from the ones given. In fact, you may have thought of a more ingenious solution. The case is one more illustration of the classic scientific method. The goal is to explain the phenomena. It first requires careful observations. Hypotheses are then needed to account for them. The hypotheses must then be tested against the empiric evidence to examine their validity. A scientist does not regard guesses about the explanation as sufficient.

Recognize that the four hypotheses above are representative of four common approaches to any problem in general. In a broader form, you will encounter them time and again. One says the difficulty is not with the evidence, but with the problem itself. Another says the problem is only apparent because accidental factors have prevented the discovery of its answer. Another says the answer is already known, but misinterpreted as something else. The last says the evidence is correct and should be taken as simply representing the way things are or were. A complication is that the correct hypothesis may be one which no one has yet suggested. For that matter, the explanation could well be some combination of both known and unknown causes.

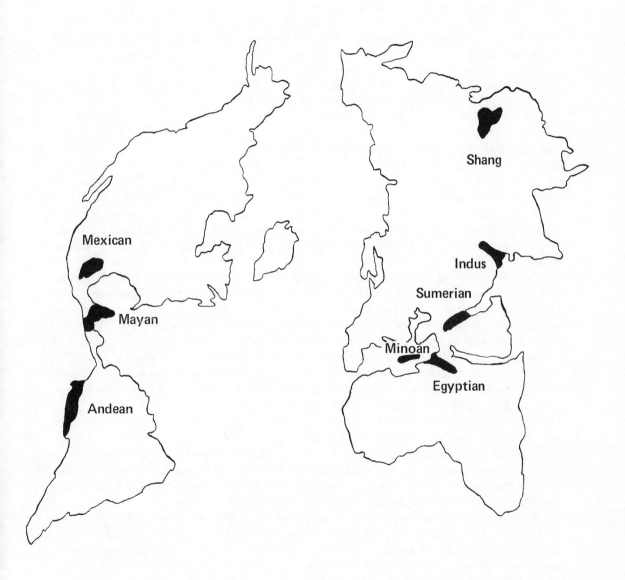

CHAPTER 7

Centers of
Early Civilization

To be *civilized* in popular conversation means to have politeness, urbanity, gentility, and good taste. To an anthropologist, it has nothing to do with virtue, but does represent a general state of cultural evolution. Civilization is a late occurrence in human history; the earliest ones began only about 6000 years ago. Furthermore, they did not spring up overnight and still do not comprise the social organization of all the world's people at the present time.

This chapter begins with a short survey of the rise of civilization. An exercise is chosen to acquaint you with the number system and calendar of the Classic Maya. A large number of early civilizations have existed, and your professor will probably not have sufficient time to discuss any of them in detail. Therefore, we want to complement the lectures with a specific illustration. In addition, you should discover that many of the theological, social, and scientific achievements of early civilizations were sometimes as highly organized as those of today.

ARCHAEOLOGICAL STAGES OF EVOLUTION

We should first clarify two concepts used to organize the archaeological record: *tradition* and *stage.* The former term implies a persistent way of making or doing things. An example would be the hand-axe tradition of the Lower Paleolithic. All kinds of people persisted in making hand axes over a long period of time. *Stage,* on the other hand, means a more general state of evolutionary development. An example would be the Mesolithic stage with its entire assemblage of artifacts and adaptations.

Perhaps an invented case will make the meanings clearer. Suppose we were interested in the history of the automobile, and excavated a junkyard to give us the raw information. The rubbish for historical reconstruction would consist of all sorts of chrome, body parts, gears, windowpanes, and so forth. It would be convenient to have some way to organize it. Distinguishing different traditions would be one way. We might be able to recognize several traditions, for example, Ford, Pontiac, and Volkswagen. Yet, another method of classification is to establish overall developmental patterns independent of the particular traditions involved. For instance, one might identify the Crank, Starter, Streamline, and Catalytic Converter Stages. Each of the various traditions or brands would follow about the same pattern of evolution through all of these.

Anthropologists often divide human history into four stages: Paleolithic, Mesolithic, Neolithic, and Civilization. The first two were briefly described in chapter 4.

Neolithic literally means "New Stone" Age. It was originally defined by the presence of pottery and stone implements made by grinding. It soon became recognized that such minor innovations were not very meaningful in relation to a total life-style. At the present, most archaeologists prefer to use farming and village life as the characteristics of Neolithic peoples everywhere.

It is not known exactly how and when farming and village life first originated. The main reason for this is the obvious marginality between pure food collecting and the growing of food to some small extent. Nonetheless, it is not difficult to imagine how farming could have developed from gathering. Seeds have long been used for human food, and they can be collected from wild plants. Some of the fruits and seeds are bound to be dropped and accidentally buried around a favorite campsite. As the new plants spring up, they will be recognized as a potential food source. Some care, watering, and cultivation might be given. Eventually, one ends up with small fields which need to be watched and tended in order to supplement the hunting and gathering which still continues. Saving some of the seeds for deliberate planting is the next step. Logically, a person would save the seeds from the plants with the most desirable characteristics, such as large yield and nonshattering seedpods. This introduces a process of selective breeding in which the plants eventually become very different from their wild ancestors. Some (corn, for example) may even become dependent upon man for propagation. It is not only the changed human interaction with plants that is important, but also the necessity for maintaining the crop. This makes demands for more or less permanently settling in place. With an increasing population, the campsites may grow into villages and the villages finally into cities.

In hunting for game animals, young offspring are sometimes found with their mothers. The infants (just as today) could be captured and saved for some future meal. This circumstance undoubtedly happened many times among hunters and gatherers, so that at least the idea of keeping animals must be very old. There is, however, no evidence of deliberately keeping herds until about 10,000 years ago. The same process of selection applied to plants can likewise be applied to animals. The cattle, sheep, and dogs of today, for example, are much modified from the original wild species.

The specifics of domestication varied in different parts of the world. Table 7.1 lists some of the approximate dates and places of origin for several important plants and animals.

TABLE 7.1
Early Records of Domesticates

ANIMAL/PLANT	LOCATION	DATES B.C.
Sheep	Iraq	8500
Dog	Idaho	8500
Goat	Iran	7500
Pig	Near East	7000
Llama	Peru	3500
Camel	Central Asia	3000
Horse	Southwest Russia	3000
Chicken	India	2000
Cat	Egypt	1600
Barley	Near East	7000
Wheat	Near East	7000
Squash	Mexico	7000
Beans	Peru	6000
Corn	Mexico	5500
Millet	China	5000

When does a farming community evolve into a civilization? What is civilization anyway? This is a straightforward question with a vague answer. The reason is that different people use the same word but mean different things by it. Many base their definitions upon some combination of characteristics, and in some parts of the world, not all of the characteristics are found. Defining a civilization is an arbitrary judgment. Most commonly, it is said to exist whenever a group of people have cities.

All right. When does a town grow into a city? It's like asking when a boy or girl becomes a man or woman.

The archaeological record indicates that Neolithic settlements first happened in the Middle East. About 10,000 years ago this certainly began to happen. At least by 7000 B.C., the farming-village way of life was well established. An example is the well-known site of Jarmo in Iraq. Some 9000 years past, farmers at Jarmo were growing wheat and barley and living in a permanent location with about 20 mud houses and perhaps 150 people. Jarmo was no metropolis by present urban standards.

However, at about the same time and toward the southwest, the scale of things would be greater. The ownership of the modern city of Jericho is presently being disputed by Israel and Jordan. It has been occupied for a long time—more than 12,000 years. A large spring with abundant water did (and still does) make it an oasis surrounded by desert. By 8000 B.C., the population probably numbered around 2000 and the inhabitants were constructing elaborate towers, ditches, and walls. Was Jericho an early civilization? If not, it came pretty close.

Anthropologists often examine societies sufficiently far along in the process of cultural evolution that everyone agrees they represent civilizations. There are a number of these which, for the most part, developed independently. Eight of them are located on the map at the beginning of the chapter. Notice that several were focused on river system irrigation: Egypt on the Nile, Sumeria between the Tigris and Euphrates, Indus on the Indus, and Shang on the Yellow. One, the Minoan, occupied the well-watered island of Crete, but even it was influenced by the river-based economy of Egypt.

New World civilizations occurred in three regions. One of these is the Valley of Mexico. It is a high, fairly dry plateau with a number of large lakes that were used for irrigation until Porfio Diaz began to drain them. Officially, the reason for draining them was mosquito control, but rumors of underwater Aztec treasure surely gave another incentive. The Aztec society was actually only the latest in a series of Mexican civilizations. At Teotihuacan, for example, a huge urban center reached its climax contemporaneously with the Roman Empire.

Other American civilizations originated further south. Mayan centers first began in the tropical rain forest of the Guatemalan highlands. Later, their civilization came to occupy the Yucatan peninsula. A series of civilizations developed in the Andes mountains, the last of them representing a political power popularly known as Incan.

All of these societies had some characteristics in common, although the specific forms varied extensively. Some of the most important include the following:

1. Monumental public architecture. This required construction by large numbers of people. Towers, pyramids, palaces, ball courts, and temples are examples.

2. Urban centers. This normally means cities with thousands of people. Some of the cities were, however, ceremonial centers serving the needs of a rural periphery.

3. Systems of notation. In all cases save one, writing was practiced. The exception was Peru. However, these people did have a record-keeping device called *quipu*. It consisted of tying cords together and served much the same purpose as writing.

4. A class- or caste-structured society. Social equality did not exist in any early civilization. All of them had slaves. Beyond the slave status, a hierarchy of citizens were stratified from commoner to noble to king.

5. Specialized economic groups. In primitive societies, there is always some division of labor if by nothing else than age and sex. Different people do different things. Civilizations take this to an extreme with complex classes of specialization in which the status and role of individuals depends, in part, upon their occupations, which come to be full-time activities. Some examples include artisans, priests, scribes, farmers, and poets.

6. "Science." We include this category with reservation since science in the modern sense has different philosophical underpinnings than existed among early civilizations. However, the overall subject matter has been the same for centuries upon centuries. All civilizations have codified bodies of knowledge maintained by specialists and related to natural phenomena. Especially important to early civilizations were astronomy, mathematics, and calendrics.

7. Warfare. Only the weapons have changed. All civilizations at one time or another have had military defense or aggression. A war to an anthropologist is not a skirmish or a feud. It involves a collective strategy fought by massive armies directed by generals.

We have selected the Maya for closer examination. Physically, they are small people, the men averaging some 5 feet in stature. Their heads are round and their noses distinctively prominent. The present population size is greater than 2 million and at least 1 million individuals must have participated in their former civilization. There is no mystery about where they came from, since they have lived in the same region for thousands of years.

This region (mostly Guatemala and the Yucatan) is about the size of Oregon. Part of it is mountainous rain forest. As one goes toward the Yucatan coast, rainfall diminishes, and the terrain is flatter. This latter territory is hot, dry, and covered with scrubby brush. The ground is underlain by limestone, and the result is karst topography. Rainwater dissolves the limestone to create underground caverns and deep sinkholes. Such sinkholes (cenotes) formed natural wells and became places of religious significance and sacrifice.

Mayan does not refer to a single language, such as English or Sanskrit. At least six different groups of languages existed, and more than 25 major dialectical varieties have been described. Many of the present-day Maya speak one or more of these in addition to Spanish. However, a large segment speak Mayan only. Some of the most important present languages include *Yucatec,* or Mayan proper, with about 300,000 speakers; *Kiče,* over 400,000; *Kakčikel,* about 300,000; and *Mam,* about 100,000.

Most of the people were rural peasants and remain so today. The principal crop was maize. Horticulture was carried out by the slash-and-burn method. This technique involves burning a patch of forest and planting a crop in the resultant clearing. After a few seasons, the plot would be abandoned, and a new one started.

Rural villages were linked to ceremonial centers. Although these were often called cities, they were generally not occupied except by a small number of priests and rulers. In the Postclassic, nonetheless, some actual cities were built. One of them at Mayapán was fortified and served an urban population of about 12,000.

Ceremonial centers were the focuses of religion and trade. Their most striking features were steep-sided pyramids. They formed the base for a small temple on the top. Unlike Egypt, the pyramids (with at least one exception) did not serve as burial tombs. Plazas, causeways, and ball courts were also constructed. Tall stone monoliths (stelae) were erected as historical markers. These, and much of the architecture, were covered with intricate and elaborate sculpture.

Religion was highly organized around gods and calendrical associations. Priests had the responsibility of manipulating and appeasing the gods for public service. The scheduling of events (such as corn planting) depended on the priests determining the proper time. This was done by noting the associated gods for any particular day. The *chac* deities were especially important since they provided rain for the fields. On market and ceremonial days, thousands of spectators gathered to watch religious rites and deadly serious ballgames and to trade their goods for artisans' products.

The high point of Mayan civilization occurred between A.D. 300 and 900. After this latter date, the priests lost much of their former power, warfare became more common, architecture and art degenerated, and human sacrifice was introduced on a much larger scale. In the southern half of the Mayan area, civilization virtually collapsed. In Yucatan, it continued under Toltec influence. The Spaniards landed in 1511, and the last military resistance to them came in 1697.

EXERCISE: THE MAYAN CALENDAR AND NUMBER SYSTEM

The Numbers

The purpose of a calendar is to record the passage of time. This requires some means of counting. Our Hindu-Arabic system is decimal, and the numbers are written horizontally. Thus, the number 362 means two units of ones, six units of tens, and three units of hundreds. The Maya wrote their numbers vertically, with the smallest units at the bottom rather than toward the right. Note that the direction of writing is merely an arbitrary convention, and if we wished, we could do the same as the Maya.

For example: 1   7   8
             0 + 6 = 6
             1   2   3

Instead of: 101
            +762
             863

In addition to this difference of direction, the Mayan number system was vigesimal. This means that it uses a base of 20 rather than 10. In such a base, the first unit is equal to 1, the next is 20 (20 X 1), followed by 400 (20 X 20), 8000 (20 X 400), and so on.

The Maya needed only three symbols to represent any number. These symbols were a dot for a value of 1, a bar for a value of 5, and a shell sign ( ) to indicate an empty space in a position.

First, examine the following equivalents up to 5.

Hindu-Arabic		Mayan
1	=	.
2	=	..
3	=	...
4	=	....
5	=	_____

What happens when we count to 6? Place a dot over the bar, and continue.

6 = __.__   9 = __....__
7 = __..__   10 = ══
8 = __...__   11 = ══̇

Until we arrive at 19, which is ....
                                ══

To ensure that you understand, write the following numbers:

17 =   14 =

The answers are __..__ and __....__ respectively. Ask the instructor for assistance if your responses were not correct.

Numbers between 20 and 399 require placement in the second position. Note the value of the positions below.

Position	Numerical Value
5	160,000
4	8,000
3	400
2	20
1	1

The number 20 requires only a single dot in the second position. Observe that the position must be known. Otherwise, a single dot could be confused with 1, 20, 400, and so forth. The Maya solved this problem with the shell sign space filler. Twenty is therefore written as or one dot over a shell. This means there is one unit of 20, nothing for any higher position, and that the lowest position is blank.

Some examples using the second position are given below.

```
    _____    =  5 units of 20
+  <shell>   =  0 units of 1        = 100
    =

    __..__   =  12 units of 20
+  __.__     =  6 units of 1        = 246
```

All of the higher positions use the same pattern. To illustrate, 40,406 is indicated.

_____	= 5 units of 8,000	= 40,000
.	= 1 unit of 400	= 400
⟨⊙⟩	= 0 units of 20	= 0
_._	= 6 units of 1	= 6

For practice, try converting 2001 and 158,777. Remember that you must have a shell glyph for blank spaces. Check your results with the answers at the end of the chapter.

Calculations are not difficult. To add, for example, sum the numbers horizontally, and carry remainders if the position values are exceeded. In the following calculation, 25 is added to 140. Note that the answer (equal to 165) is obtained by the simple process of summing the units toward the right.

If you are interested, try determining the rules for subtraction, multiplication, and division.

The Calendar

The Maya required a number system capable of representing any given quantity and calculation. This was necessary in order to relate their lives to the passage of time. In our society, the calendar has (despite the current fad with astrology) lost most of its original magical and religious associations. This was not the case among the Maya; every day was a combination of gods. Some of the gods had benevolent qualities, others were destructive. Many were in control of natural forces of vital concern, such as fertility and rain. The interaction of the gods on a day-to-day basis supplied guidance for social and individual decisions. It was thus extremely important to keep track of the supernatural succession as the days passed.

The significance of their calendar has been eloquently described by J. Eric Thompson (1954):

The great theme of Maya civilization is the passage of time—the wide concept of the mystery of eternity and the narrower concept of the divisions of time into their equivalents of centuries, years, months, and days. The rhythm of time enchanted the Maya; the never ending flow of days from the eternity of the future into the eternity of the past filled them with wonder. Calculations far into the past or lesser probings of the future occur in many a Maya hieroglyphic text. On one stela at the city of Quirigua accurate computation sweeps back over ninety million years; on another stela at the same site the date reached is some four hundred million years ago. These are actual computations stating correctly day and month positions, and are comparable to calculation in our calendar giving the month positions on which Easter would have fallen at equivalent distances in the past. The brain reels at such astronomical figures, yet these reckonings were of sufficient frequency and importance to require special hieroglyphs for their transcription, and they were made nearly a thousand years before Archbishop Ussher had placed the creation of the world at 4004 B.C. This was an appraisal of the ages which would have been utterly inconceivable to us today, had not our minds been conditioned to their vastness by the writings of the astronomers and geologists of the nineteenth century.

To commemorate events, the Maya often erected stone monuments called *stelae*. These have dates inscribed upon them, and archaeologists are able to convert them into a corresponding date in our own calendar. This gives a highly accurate means of reconstructing cultural history. The next exercise will demonstrate how the dates are converted. In actuality, there are some minor complexities which we will ignore.

One must first recognize the Maya had several types of calendars; two of the most important were for the sacred year and the solar year. The sacred year was an almanac which repeated itself every 260 days. On the other hand, the solar calendar reflected the length of time for the annual cycle of the sun. These two calendars coincided (with their starting points again matched) once in

52 years. This occurrence of the calendar round every 52 years was a dreadful circumstance marking a time of continence, fasting, and sacrifice to ensure that the world would continue.

The name for one day is *kin*. Twenty days comprise one *uinal*. It took 18 *uinal* (one *tun* or 360 days) to approximate the solar year. A problem arises with all calendars, since the yearly cycle of the sun is not divisible into a whole number; it is approximately 365.2422 days. Our Gregorian calendar reaches 365 by a combination of 12 months of varying lengths. The 0.24 day residue is compensated for by leap years—adding an extra day in every year exactly divisible by 4 (as in 1776) except in centenary years not exactly divisible by 400 (as in 1900).

The Mayan solution was somewhat more elegant. Each month had 20 days (one *uinal*). The closest approximation to the true year in multiples of 20 is 18. Eighteen *uinal* (360 days) fall short by 5.24 days. The Maya corrected by adding a five-day period (*uayeb*), which was considered to be an unlucky time. The priest-astronomers further corrected by marginal calculations with the 0.2422-day residue. The result was a calendar which was more accurate than that used by Europeans at the time of the Mayan conquest.

The following table will help you to convert.

20 *katun*	=	1 *baktun*	=	144,000 days	
20 *tun*	=	1 *katun*	=	7,200 days	
18 *uinal*	=	1 *tun*	=	360 days	
				+ 5 = 1 year	
20 *kin*	=	1 *uinal*	=	20 days = 1 month	
1 *kin*			=	1 day	

While the Maya had names for even larger units of time, we will not need them.

Let's try a problem converting our own calendar first. An important event happened in American history on July 4, 1776. How would we indicate this in the Mayan method?

We first begin with a starting date. In the European tradition, this date is the birth of Jesus. A minor problem exists since the exact day and year of the event is not known. The 25th day of December was selected at a much later time. We, therefore, do not know exactly how many days have passed. European calendar reforms in the sixteenth century also add complexity. We will simply take July 4, 1776, as representing so many days since zero.

This is the first step. Count the number of days. Begin with the first of January of the year indicated. To help you with this, the month days are

January −31	May −31	September −30
February −28 or 29	June −30	October −31
March −31	July −31	November −30
April −30	August −31	December −31

Note that July 4 was the 186th day of the year. (Since 1776 was a leap year, February had 29 days.) To the previous sum add the number of days which have passed for all the previous years. There were 1775 complete previous years, and if we round the length of each to 365.24, this amounts to 648,301. Adding 186 to this, the total is 648,487.

All that remains is successive division. Start with the largest Mayan unit required and divide by that number. Do not worry about fractions. Simply set the residue aside.

The mechanics are shown below.

Days from zero to July 4, 1776 = 648,487

648,487/144,000 =	4 baktun	+	72,487 days remaining
72,487/7,200	= 10 katun	+	487 days remaining
487/360 + 5	= 1 tun + uayeb	+	122 days remaining
122/20	= 6 uinal	+	2 days remaining
2/1	= 2 kin	+	0 days remaining

And the answer is:

Scholars often rewrite the dates in a form more suitable for contemporary books. This involves Arabic numbers followed by periods. Thus, 4.10.1.6.2. is the conventional way to designate the Mayan notation of July 4, 1776. What is 7.0.3.? (Seven *tun,* zero *uinal,* and three *kin.*)

Bear in mind that we took the birth of Christ as the starting date in this exercise. The Maya, of course, did not; their starting date began about 5,000 years ago, probably in 3113 B.C.

One is normally interested in converting Mayan to Gregorian time rather than vice versa. To illustrate, let us take the date which marks the beginning of the highest development of Mayan civilization. It is 8.12.14.8.15.

Multiplying the value of each unit times the number of days it represents, we have

8 *baktun*	X	144,000 days	=	1,152,000 days
12 *katun*	X	7,200 days	=	86,400 days
14 *tun*	X	365 days	=	5,110 days
8 *uinal*	X	20 days	=	160 days
15 *kin*			=	15 days

And this means that a total of 1,243,685 days have passed from the start. The most commonly accepted starting date is 3113 B.C. Each one of the solar years had 365.24 days. Thus 1,136,992 days passed in that time. The Mayan date recorded is greater than 3113 years by 106,693 days. To obtain the number of years, divide by 365.24, and the answer is 292 A.D.

The end of the Classic period of Mayan civilization is regarded to have occurred when they abandoned this long-count notation in favor of a short-count abbreviated system. The most recent long-count date on a stela is 10.3.0.0.0. This began a new phase in their society, and the Maya were eventually overwhelmed by foreign invaders. Taking 10.3.0.0.0. as the end of the Classic period, what year did this start to happen?

Answers to problems on page 83:

2001 = _____

158,777 = · · · ·

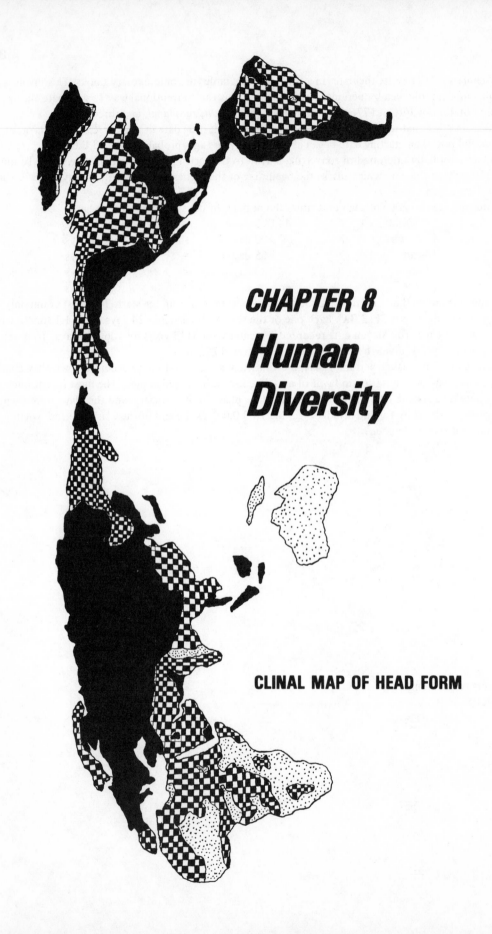

CHAPTER 8
Human Diversity

CLINAL MAP OF HEAD FORM

Physical anthropologists focus their attention on human biological variation. They are concerned with how and why such variation originated. They also want to know how and why it varies at the present time. This chapter describes methods of classification and contains some exercises to illustrate a few forms of biological difference.

Racial taxonomy is one method of organizing the variation. Such classifications are typological; they place individuals into different groups on the basis of traits which races are thought to share in common. Since human variation actually intergrades from one group to another, racial taxonomy is not an accurate reflection of how variations are distributed in reality. The method is artificial and subjective. There is no agreement upon the number of human races, and many of the world's individuals and populations do not neatly fit any racial scheme of classification. Some anthropologists argue that human races do not exist. They emphasize gradual rather than discrete changes from one group to the next.

A second method is populational. It classifies differences between groups on the basis of the frequency differences of various traits. These are usually relative genetic variations, such as the frequency of blood group alleles among different peoples. The objective is to distinguish breeding populations. The major problem of the populational method is that all human groups are connected by interbreeding, and the lines between different breeding populations are arbitrary. They are no more distinct than are the arbitrary divisions obtained by classifying races.

A third common approach is clinal. It deals with the distribution of the traits themselves. The method is similar to the construction of contour maps or weather maps. Lines are drawn around areas having equal frequencies of particular traits. Examine the following clinal map, which was invented for a fictional characteristic X.

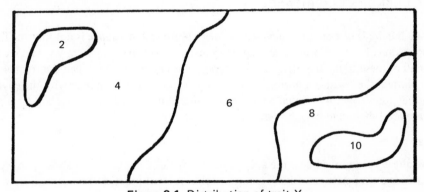

Figure 8.1. Distribution of trait X.

Note that the map is a way of summarizing the variation. The value of X was determined at a number of locations throughout the region and discovered to vary from an average of two units in some parts of the region to more than ten units in others. Lines were then drawn connecting points of equal or similar occurrence. The further apart the lines are, the slower the rate of change. Lines which are close together indicate a more rapid change in the pattern of distribution. Observe that the value of X gradually increases toward the southeast and diminishes toward the northwest. Any such gradual change in the geographical distribution of a biological trait is called a cline. The particular lines themselves (which separate areas of equal class intervals) also have names. They are called *isophenes* if the trait in question is one of unknown inheritance. Examples of such traits would be skin color or stature. If the offspring genotype can be determined, the specific lines are *isogenes*. Examples of these traits include various blood groups and types of hemoglobin. Regardless of the kind of trait, the isogenes or isophenes are analogous to isobars connecting regions of similar atmospheric pressure which you see for a daily weather report.

The clinal method is fairly objective. It may also suggest hypotheses of explanation. One can correlate the pattern of distribution with different environmental or ecological variables.

Let's take an example. People differ in the shape of their heads. Some individuals and populations have heads which are rather long and narrow. Others have heads which are almost round. The head shape varies continuously from one extreme to the other. Anthropologists have been all over the world measuring the heads of thousands of people. They usually summarize the head shape with the cephalic index. This is equal to the breadth divided by the length, with the quotient multiplied by 100. This number varies from about 65 to 90. The higher the number, the rounder the head. When the indices are plotted on a map of the world, a correlation is noted when the distribution of head shape is compared to climate. With some exceptions, mostly American Indians originally from Siberia, round heads are typically found in cold regions, and long heads are most common among peoples native to hot areas. This suggests the trait might be explained by adaptation to temperature. Since the hypothesis is further supported by physical principles showing that rounder objects lose less heat by radiation, the evidence is strong that the variation we see with head shape is in part explained by the slow evolution of the body adapting to different kinds of climates.

Plotting the clines of traits does not, however, automatically lead to an explanation. There are many characteristics in which the geographical pattern of distribution gives no clue as to why it happens to be the way it is. More over, correlations often happen between variables which do not necessarily cause each other.

The practical exercises in this chapter are for you to determine how you vary from others for a few selected characteristics. There are no written problems; it is sufficient to become familiar with the methods. Do not proceed until the instructor indicates.

TRAITS OF UNKNOWN INHERITANCE

There are hundreds of examples in which the mechanism of inheritance is not known. They include stature, skin color, hair form, nose shape, and many others—most of what you can see about a person. For all of these traits, the offspring genotype cannot be predicted. When the frequency of the traits is plotted, the result is a normal curve. Several or many genes interact with the environment to produce the observation. We will take two cases to illustrate how anthropologists measure them. These two are head shape and overall body build.

Head Shape

We have already mentioned how the average head shape of a population is a reasonably good indicator of the kind of climate to which a group is native. A short practical exercise will show you how the shape is determined.

It requires an instrument. Spreading calipers are the instruments used. Notice that they have two movable arms which spread apart. There is a crossbar between them. Note the markings on the crossbar. Each number is a division in centimeters.

All scientific measurements are metric. One centimeter equals 0.3937 inches. Each centimeter contains 10 millimeters. Note that there are 10 small lines (each one 1 millimeter in length) between the numbers marking the centimeters.

Calipers are read to the nearest millimeter. Sliding along the crossbar is a metal edge divided in the center to permit the millimeter lines to be seen. The front edge of the slide represents the distance between the caliper tips. Directly behind the slide is a set screw permitting the distance to be held in place.

Loosen the set screw if it is tight, and move the slide along the crossbar. Set the slide at 9.6 centimeters and tighten the screw. The instructor will check to see if you are reading the calipers properly.

Now that you are ready to do it, the next step is knowing what to do. Since it is extraordinarily difficult to measure your own head, we recommend working in pairs. Select a partner.

The cephalic index requires two distances: length and breadth. Landmarks on the cranium are used as reference points. Length is the space between the glabella and opisthocranion. The glabella is the most anterior point of the cranium between the brow ridges. It will be slightly above the root of the nose. The opisthocranion is the most posterior point of the head not including the external occipital protuberance. Recall from your anatomy lesson that the latter is the bump on the lower, middle back of the head. Ignore it as the most posterior point.

The best way to hold the instrument is with your fingers behind the caliper tips. Place one tip on the glabella. Rotate the rear tip of the calipers around the back of the head until you have located the maximum distance at the opisthocranion. Close the tips together (gently, please) and read the measurement. Record the centimeters and millimeters, i.e., 19.7 or whatever it is.

Breadth is the maximum distance in a transverse direction. Unless your subject has a weird head, this will be about in the middle and toward the top.

After recording each measurement, simply substitute the values into the formula.

Cephalic index = (breadth/length) 100

The only purpose of multiplying by 100 is to remove the unwieldy decimal place.

The longer your head is, the lower your cephalic index will be. Round heads have high indices. Sometimes the value of the index is separated into arbitrary categories, but they have little use except for descriptive generality.

Brachycephaly   = 82.0 and over
Mesocephaly   = 77.0 to 81.9
Dolichocephaly = 76.9 and under

What kind of head do you have? Next year's Miss America will likely be a 3—4—3 leptorrhine mesocephalic with Carabelli's pits or cusps. You're probably about the same yourself.

Body Build

Since the time of Hippocrates, scientists have had an interest in the relationship between body form and medical or psychological conditions. We are all familiar with the cultural folklore which identifies thin individuals with being smart and nervous, while fat people are jolly extroverts. More seriously, it is common knowledge that excess weight is correlated with certain physical disorders. Heart attacks and diabetes have, for example, a higher frequency with obesity.

Anthropologists, psychologists, and physicians all share a common concern of research with body bulk. It requires more standardized methods than subjective categories. Some special procedures have been devised for it. They include photographic comparisons (somatotyping), fat fold measurement, and density studies with the subjects being submersed in water.

The ponderal index is more suitable for our purpose. This index expresses the ratio between stature and the cube root of the weight. While it is a rather crude evaluation of body build, it does have more objectivity than simple statement that a person is fat, skinny, or medium.

Begin by weighing yourself. The available scales may record in pounds rather than kilograms. If this is the case, you will have to convert. Pounds are converted to kilograms by multiplying the pound weight by 0.4536.

After your weight is determined in kilograms, it has to be converted to the cube root. This is most simply done by reference (table 8.1).

TABLE 8.1
Cube Roots of Weight in Kilograms

KG	CUBE ROOT	KG	CUBE ROOT
45	3.557	75	4.217
50	3.684	80	4.309
55	3.803	85	4.397
60	3.915	90	4.481
65	4.021	95	4.563
70	4.121	100	4.642

Simple interpolation will give fairly accurate cube roots for weights not found in even multiples of five.

The next step is to have your stature determined. An anthropometer is the most commonly used device. It is a set of calipers with a very long shaft and sliding crossbars. The markings are again in centimeters and millimeters.

Have the subject stand erect. The shoulders should be rotated backward and the head facing directly forward. Shoes are preferably removed.

Hold the anthropometer behind the subject, taking care to keep the anthropometer shaft vertical. Slide the crossbar down until it rests firmly (but gently) on the top of the head. Read the stature on the instrument scale. The instructor will demonstrate the details.

All that remains is to substitute the values into the formula.

$$\text{Ponderal index} = \text{stature} / \sqrt[3]{\text{weight}}$$

The result varies from about 37 to 49; 43 is average. Heavy body builds are characterized by low indices. The higher the number, the less weight you carry relative to your height.

Within the population, differences in body build relate to a large number of factors, such as hereditary influence and diet. When means for populations around the world are plotted, heavy peoples tend to be concentrated in cold climates. The reason for this is thought to be the same as that for the cephalic index. Thin individuals have more surface area and hence radiate proportionally more of their body heat to the environment. This is advantageous in a hot area and detrimental in a cold one.

TRAITS OF KNOWN INHERITANCE

Examples of these characters include many different types of hemoglobin, haptoglobin, blood groups, PTC tasting, and hundreds of genetic disorders, such as albinism, brachydactyly, and many more. We will consider three of them: ABO blood type, taster status, and color blindness.

The blood typing exercise will take a few minutes for incubation. While this is occurring, the color blindness and taster test should be done. All of the exercises should be carefully read before performing them.

ABO Blood Groups

Obtaining a blood sample requires pricking your finger. If quickly done, it is almost physically and psychologically painless. Thousands of students have done it for themselves. *However, we do not want you to try it without supervision.* You are also in no way required to prick your finger; skip it and watch if you so desire.

First, familiarize yourself with the following basic information.

There are dozens of separate blood groups, of which the ABO system is only one. More are being discovered. Some of them are polymorphic. This means two or more of their alleles have common frequencies. Examples include Kell, Diego, Duffy, Rhesus, P, X_g, Hunter, and Henshaw. For some other blood types, virtually everyone has them (public). Others are private; almost no one has them. Both of these latter cases are idiomorphic. This means that one kind of allele is extremely common, and all the others are extremely rare. Mutation is often used to explain the presence of idiomorphs. Polymorphs cannot be explained by mutation alone, since two or more alleles are common.

There is much confusion with the blood types of an individual. Hospitals, for instance, often record types as O^- or B^+ (ABO letters followed by a plus or a minus). Only the letters A, B, O, or AB refer to the ABO group. the positive or negative is an indication of the presence or absence of a particular allele in the Rhesus system (allele D). It is unrelated to the ABO type.

You must be aware of antigen-antibody reactions. An antigen is a substance eliciting the production of antibodies. Suppose you are stung by a bee. It injects foreign proteins (antigens) into the blood stream. Your body reacts to their presence by producing antibodies. They normally destroy or inactivate the foreign substance. They protect, but may kill us in the process. Paradoxical? Yes, but the antibodies have no way of distinguishing desirable invasions from bad ones. Without the antibodies, microorganisms and foreign material could multiply and wreak havoc with the body's functions. Evolution has provided us with several means of defense, one of which is antibody formation. Yet the same process of protection is also the major problem with tissue or organ transplants. They are rejected as foreign even though the person may die without them. Certain drugs do suppress a part of the reaction, but the same drugs also reduce resistance to infection. Thus, even though the transplant is surgically successful, the patient might still die from inhibition of the natural defenses.

ABO antibodies are somewhat unusual since they are naturally occurring. They circulate in the blood stream even though no foreign blood has ever been injected. If this is the case, then why is anyone alive? Why don't the antibodies react with a person's own blood?

The answer is that the antibodies are not the right kind.

We also need to explain this. Blood is not a uniform tissue. You may think of it as a homogeneous red fluid. Don't. It's more like a bowl of straw-colored soup. Floating in the soup are many different kinds of cells, some of which contain hemoglobin. These are the red blood cells (erythrocytes), and their red color comes from iron within the hemoglobin, which transports oxygen to all of the cells.

The stock of the soup is the plasma or serum. These two words do have different technical meanings, but we can conveniently ignore the difference. The antigens are present on the surface of the red blood cells. The antibodies float along in the serum.

In the ABO system, there are three of each. The antigens are arbitrarily designated A, B, and O. The corresponding antibodies are -A, -B, and -O. However, no antiserum has yet been discovered for -O, and we may regard it as nothing for our purpose.

These permit the detection of four ABO types: A, B, AB, and O. These come from three alleles: I^A, I^B, and I^O. (The capital letter I stands for isoagglutinin.) The thoughtful reader will surely note that this cannot be the case since three alleles in combinations of two's will give more than four genotypes. Reward yourself if you recognized the problem.

So, let's explain this too. The I^O allele cannot yet be determined when it occurs in combination with I^A or I^B. This is another way to say that both I^A and I^B are dominant to I^O. The last allele can be recognized only in the homozygous state (or sometimes known by pedigree studies).

Even with this limitation, how can blood types be detected in the laboratory?

Think about it. What have we told you?

1. Antigens and corresponding antibodies produce a reaction when put together.

2. Antigens are on the surface of the red blood cells and antibodies are in the serum.

Problem: What kind of antigens and antibodies does any particular person have?

Solution: Mix the red blood cells from different people with the known serum from different people, and see what kind of reactions happen.

Your solution was brilliant.

It is now a matter of procedure.

Antigens react with antibodies in different ways, but in regard to blood typing, you can detect a reaction by agglutination. The antibodies cause the antigens to clump together. This is not clotting, a separate process in which the serum protects itself from leaking excessively from a wound.

Now refer to table 8.2.

Reference to table 8.2 will tell you what reactions to expect whenever a particular antiserum is mixed with any particular ABO antigen on the red blood cells. Thus, if serum from a B individual is mixed with red blood cells from an A individual, agglutination will occur. If serum from a B individual, however, is mixed with the blood from an O individual, no agglutination will happen. This is the basis of the test you will be performing.

1. Obtain a microscope slide.

2. Place one drop of anti-A serum on the left side of the slide. Place one drop of anti-B serum on the right side.

TABLE 8.2

Phenotypes, Genotypes, Antigens, and Antibodies in the ABO System

POSSIBLE GENOTYPE	OBSERVED PHENOTYPE	ANTIGENS	ANTIBODIES
$I^A I^A$	A	A	Anti-B
$I^A I^0$	A	A	Anti-B
$I^B I^B$	B	B	Anti-A
$I^B I^0$	B	B	Anti-A
$I^A I^B$	AB	AB	None
$I^0 I^0$	O	None	Anti-A, Anti-B

3. Obtain a sterile, disposable lancet and an alcohol-saturated cotton pad.
4. Scrub the fingertip to be punctured with the pad.
5. Remove the lancet from its container, taking care not to contaminate the tip or the scrubbed finger.
6. Make a quick and firm puncture of the finger. (The region slightly to the side of the ball is less sensitive than the ball itself.)
7. Discard the lancet. Do not use it more than once or for any other person.
8. Stroke downward on the punctured fingertip to force the drop of blood out. (If too much pressure is applied, the blood may not flow.)
9. Let one drop of blood fall into the drop of anti-A and another into the anti-B. (This may not work quite so easily. If so, use a toothpick to wipe off some of the blood, and place the sample in the anti-A.) Do the same for anti-B with another toothpick.
10. Mix the blood sample and antiserum with the toothpicks, taking care not to mix one antiserum with the other.
11. Let the mixture stand at room temperature for 10 minutes. While it is incubating, proceed to the color blindness and taster tests.
12. Observe the results after the period of incubation. Record your blood type.

If agglutination occurs, the red cells will be clumped together in small masses. They will float in the clear antiserum. If no agglutination occurs, the mixture will have a homogeneous and cloudy appearance.

TABLE 8.3

Interpretation of Blood Tests

REACTION WITH ANTI-A	REACTION WITH ANTI-B	ABO BLOOD TYPE
+	−	A
−	+	B
−	−	O
+	+	AB

Agglutination is indicated by a positive sign. A minus sign is used to mean no reaction. Refer to figure 8.2.

Hospitals and researchers use more sophisticated procedures. If you are interested, advanced classes in physical anthropology usually teach them. They are all based upon the antigen-antibody reaction. The principle upon which the test is based is what you should remember. If you are type B, for example, the anti-B serum reacts with your B antigens and causes the agglutination. The anti-A serum does not since you have no anti-A antigens.

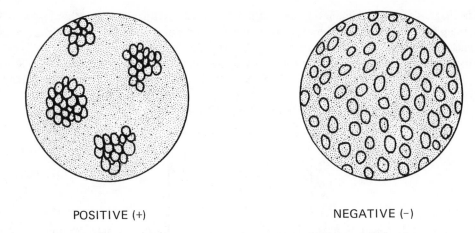

POSITIVE (+)   NEGATIVE (−)

Figure 8.2. Positive and negative serological agglutination.

Why do people have different blood types? Why are there differences in frequency for the same type among different populations? What is their adaptive significance?

These are all questions which anthropologists have tried to answer. As yet, no simple explanation has been proposed. Moreover, the answer for one blood group may be entirely different for another. We will mention some of the associations which have been discovered.

The ABO antigens are thought to have a great antiquity. The evidence for this is that the polymorphism also exists among other hominoids. Perhaps, their adaptive significance relates to something in the remote past which no longer operates today. If this is the case, we will probably never recognize it.

It is likely that the antigens have digestive functions. They are more concentrated in such tissue. Correlations have also been suggested between ABO frequencies and dietary differences among ethnic groups.

There are also statistical associations between blood types and disease. A individuals have higher occurrences of pernicious anemia and stomach cancer. O individuals are somewhat more likely to get ulcers.

Recent studies suggest that malaria may play a role in the distributions. As strange as it may sound, mosquitos prefer to land on people of particular ABO types.

Extreme differences in allelic frequency are less common than expected among different groups. It has been suggested that the reason for this is that heterozygotes have a selective advantage.

On the other hand, blood group incompatibilities select against heterozygosity. If the parents have different types, their offspring may be spontaneously aborted because of the antigen-antibody reaction within the fetus. Such incompatibilities are more widely known for the Rh system, but they can in fact be even more severe with ABO groups.

Perhaps all of these circumstances are involved in explaining the variation. Almost certainly, there are others, which are unknown. It's a fascinating puzzle.

Color Blindness

Color blindness is not a single trait, since several different forms of it are known to exist. The most extreme (but also very rare) form is the total inability to recognize color (achromatopsia or monochromatism). Individuals with this condition are only able to distinguish difference in brightness. Their impressions of the world are similar to black and white photography.

Less severe variations occur with distinguishing hues. There are differences not only with the specific colors involved, but also in the degree of severity. You will be screening yourself for red-green and blue-yellow deficiencies. These are the most common forms.

The diagnosis of color blindness is done with pseudoisochromatic plates. For the greatest reliability, the plates should only be shown by an experienced examiner and with standardized procedure and lighting conditions. We will save time with a less rigorous method.

First examine demonstration plate I. Unless you are totally color-blind, you will see an X symbol in the upper right corner and also an O symbol in the lower left corner. The plate is thus marked as follows:

Demonstration Plate I

	X
O	

Next, inspect demonstration plate II. Mark what you see in the appropriate location.

Demonstration Plate II

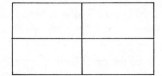

You should have put a Δ symbol in the upper left corner and an X in the lower left. Ask the instructor for guidance if it was not marked correctly.

The only symbols used in the plates are X's, O's, and Δ's. If you see any of these as the plates are passed to you, mark their positions as you see them. They may occur in any combination of symbols.

Now compare your results with the responses of individuals with normal color vision. These are printed upside down at the end of the chapter.

If you marked a different result in either of the first two test plates, you probably have a blue-yellow defect. Red-green defects are indicated by any disparity in plates 3, 4, 5, and 6.

The degree of deficiency may be tested with additional plates. If you are interested, you may obtain the test booklet from the instructor. Follow the directions carefully.

Among males of European descent, the most common red-green blindness occurs (in some degree or another) in about 1 man in 12. However, only about 1 woman in 200 has a similar defect.

The anthropology of color vision is quite interesting. Hunters and gatherers have the lowest rates of defects, and the proportion increases among those living in more complex societies. The reason for this is believed to be the disadvantage of color blindness in the collecting of food.

Tasting Status

Virtually everyone has the ability to taste, which is in part dependent upon the ability to smell. We do not, however, receive exactly the same impression of the substances around us. There are some materials which only some people can taste. Even with this, some individuals are able to taste them at a lower concentration than others.

The closely related substances phenythiocarbamide and phenythiourea are examples. The inheritance of the ability to taste them is more complicated than is ordinarily presented. At least two pairs of alleles are required to account for the inheritance. However, most of the variation is determined by one gene with two alleles. Let's call them T and t.

We will do the most simple test possible. You will be given a plastic squeeze bottle containing the PTC solution in a standard concentration. Squirt a few drops on your finger. If it has a bitter taste, you are a taster. If it has no taste, you are probably a nontaster. If you are a taster, you'll know it. If not, you may wish to sample some of the stronger concentrations.

Taster status is another case with no simple explanation for its variation. Nontasters are more likely to have goiter than tasters. Perhaps tasters have some slight selective advantage in being able to detect bitter-tasting substances known to suppress the activity of the thyroid gland.

EXERCISE: METHODS OF EVALUATION

Study the lesson; determine and record the following traits for yourself.

A. Cephalic index: _____

B. Ponderal index: _____

C. ABO blood type: _____

D. Color blindness test results: _____

E. Taster status:_____

Answers to the color blindness screening:

Plate 1: X upper left, O lower left

Plate 2: △ upper right, O lower left

Plate 3: △ upper left, X lower left

Plate 4: △ upper left, O lower left

Plate 5: O lower left

Plate 6: X upper right

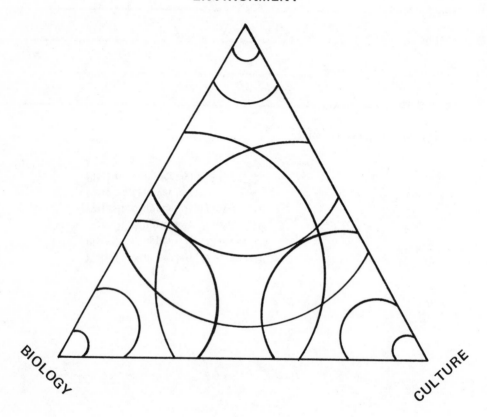

ENVIRONMENT

BIOLOGY

CULTURE

CHAPTER 9
Cultural Biology

Anthropology is the study of human variation through time and space for social and biological characteristics. Chapter 9 is intended to illustrate how these classes of phenomena interact to produce the human as a whole. Some statistical ways of analyzing the variation are described. The exercise relates the variability within populations to the interpretation of fossil remains.

EXAMPLES OF BIOCULTURAL INTERACTION

Why are we the way we are? What are we in the first place? The scientific answer is short, sweet, and sweeping: we are the product of ecological adaptation in the present and the past. Such grand generalities do provide a direction of inquiry, but seldom satisfy one's curiosity for specifics. Nonetheless, it is the broadest way to begin.

Any human variation (from skin color to drug addiction to language to politics) is part of an interactive process between the natural environment, cultural learning, and biological capacity.

This does not mean that all three are equally significant toward the explanation of particulars. It is convenient to visualize a triangle with biology, culture, and environment at the apexes. The natural environment—including climate, topography, physical laws, flora, and fauna—forms the backdrop for human evolution. The cultural and biological apexes form our means of adaptation.

Any particular variable could be plotted within such a triangle according to the degree of influence from each. For example, the structure of a person's language bears little, if any, relationship to the environment or biological disposition. As you know, you could speak English or Japanese anywhere in the world and do so regardless of your stature, skin color, sex, or biochemical metabolism. The form of language thus falls far into the corner of cultural experience. The implication is that if you wish to explain why different people speak different languages, then cultural history will be a far more important source for the answer than the biological or environmental differences between speakers of Japanese or English.

Still, however, you might say that environmental and biological factors are not totally irrelevant. After all, no person would speak either English or Japanese if they had the vocal anatomy of a frog. As the result of common biological ancestry, all humans share a similar type of vocal anatomy which limits the kinds of sounds we can produce in speaking any language.

There are three classes of biological influence upon behavior: universal, idiomorphic, and polymorphic.

The first class is shared by people everywhere. It will not explain differences between populations, but it does relate to the behavior of the species. For instance, the ancestors of primates had tails and so do most primates today, with the exception of apes and people. Suppose we were more typical mammals and had retained tails during the evolutionary process. Clothing styles, poetry, insurance policies, athletic events—all these and more would have a different form.

The shape of our artifacts (from typewriters, coffee cups, guns, and computers) are all designed for the particular kind of grasping, five-fingered hand which came to us from our biological ancestry. Likewise, our patterns of mating, kinship, and family organization in part reflect two nontypical reproductive processes.

Human females are sexually receptive through the reproductive period and have a menstrual rather than an estrus cycle. What if we had restricted breeding seasons? The month of June? The tenth of December? Whatever the time, our behavior and social institutions would be different at that time than otherwise.

There are several points to remember about biological universals. In the first place, they are unlearned and, in that sense, noncultural. We come into the world as infants already equipped with a substantial behavioral repertoire—sucking, breathing, crying, grasping. Throughout our lives, the body maintains and protects itself with vegetative and reflexive actions. It sends hunger pains and sex urges.

Yet a second point is that even such basic biological functions can be modified by cultural experience. Humans are particularly adept at this, and it is not surprising given the enormous role of learned behavior in which our species specializes. Even body functions such as belching and flatulence have been adapted by some societies as a complex system of communicating appreciation. Even the type of electrochemical waves produced by the brain can be modified with practice.

Behavioral influence by biological idiomorphisms ranges from subtle to striking. We are talking about abnormal rather than universal conditions. By "abnormal" we mean less common than average. Genetic deficiencies offer the clearest examples.

Let's take a case. Nearly all individuals produce the skin pigment melanin. The genetics of melanin production is well understood. It is due to a dominant gene which occurs with a high frequency. Occasionally, people are born without the allele; that is, they are homozygous recessive, and the result is an albino phenotype. Albinos lack the presence of brownish pigment in the skin, and the eyes appear pink because the melanin does not mask the hemoglobin present within the capillaries of the eye. Albinism means that the skin cannot tan in the presence of sunlight. Bright sunlight is irritating, and the behavioral response is to stay out of it as much as possible.

With albinism, the behavioral consequence is obvious but slight. Yet with other abnormalities, it can be severe. One of the most tragic is Huntington's chorea. It is due to a dominant gene, but one whose impact is not manifest until the subject is about 30 years of age. The condition is fatal, and the process is the gradual destruction of the brain, resulting in progressive physical and mental degeneration.

Hundreds of such genetic disorders have been discovered, and their prominence as medical and social problems increases consistently as cultural evolution provides more success against the microbial and viral diseases which were so often responsible for human misery of the past.

Recent attention has focused upon chromosome abnormalities. Various mental and physical conditions, such as sterility and mental retardation, can be correlated with the type of chromosome pattern which an individual possesses.

One chromosome anomaly in particular may have consequences for aggressive behavior. This is the highly controversial case of XYY males. Recall from chapter 3 that men and women contribute equally to their offspring. An exception, however, occurs with the sex chromosomes. Normal individuals have two sex chromosomes. Their appearance is different from the remaining 22 pairs in each cell, and so they can be distinguished by microscopic examination. There are two types of sex chromosomes, a larger one designated as X and a smaller one, Y. Among females, both chromosomes are X; males have one X and one Y. The Y chromosome determines the sex of the embryo; a person is a chromosomal male whenever a Y is present. If no Y is present, the individual is female. This is true regardless of any unusual condition where the number of sex chromosomes differs from two. Examine the ordinary process depicted in figure 9.1.

But, things occasionally go wrong. It is possible for the chromosomes to be damaged. Parts may be missing or rearranged. Sometimes the entire chromosome may be either lost or doubled into a single reproductive cell. In figure 9.2 the Y chromosome occurs twice, and when the sperm carrying it combines with a normal X from the mother, the son will have two Y chromosomes for a total of 47 instead of 46. We say "son" because even a single Y makes a man. Does a double Y make a superman?

It is difficult to see how the presence of an extra Y chromosome in cells of the body would influence behavior. Yet, some have concluded that studies show associations with a range of physical and social problems—abnormal stature, violence, mental retardation, truancy, antisocial behavior, murder, rape and plunder, bizarre sexual activity, and severe acne.

Studies in prisons and mental institutions have yielded frequencies about 20 times higher than in the general population. Still, however, only 4% of the total XYY individuals are in prisons or mental institutions. The great majority are apparently as normal as anyone. Why? What internal, social, and environmental situations are involved? We do not know the answers. Moreover, scientists are now finding the conclusions of the original studies to be suspect.

The third class of biological influence consists of cases in which two or more various forms have common frequencies and in which frequencies differ among ethnic groups. Interactions have been

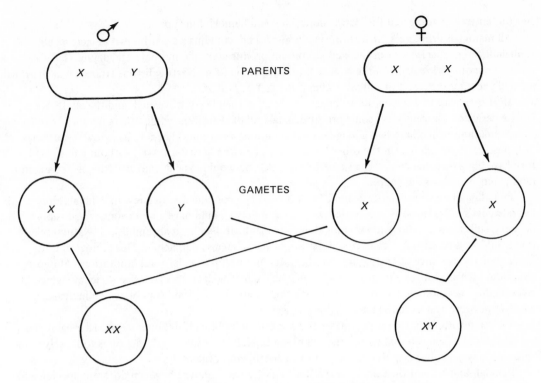

Figure 9.1. Sex chromosomes in a typical daughter and son.

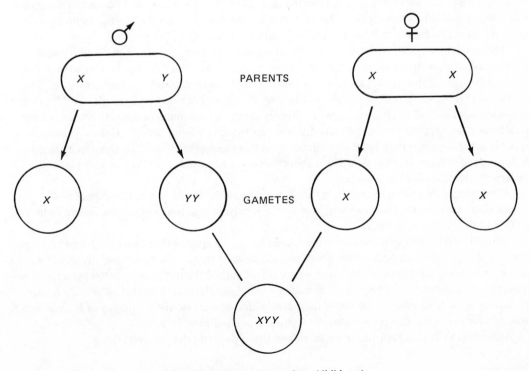

Figure 9.2. Production of an *XYY* male.

most intensively investigated for lactase deficiency and hemoglobin types.

All mammals drink milk, at least during infancy. Milk contains a sugar known as lactose, although different species vary in the lactose content produced by the mother. An enzyme (lactase) must be present to break down the lactose into a digestible form. Gastric distress (translate as diarrhea and bellyache) is the result of milk drinking if the lactase is absent.

Most mammals lose the ability to produce lactase as they become weaned, and the adults are lactase deficient. Humans vary; some produce lactase all of their lives, while others do not.

Populations which have had a long cultural tradition of dairying generally have low frequencies of lactase-deficient adults. On the other hand, groups (such as in eastern Asia) without a dairying history have higher frequencies of lactase deficiency. As you would expect, milk drinking is not a common practice among such people.

Probably all human societies around 10,000 years ago contained only a few individuals able to tolerate cow's milk. However, those that were able to do so would have a more stable food supply once the cultural adaptations for keeping domestic mammals had been accomplished. Natural selection would thus be expected to decrease the frequency of lactase deficiency. This biological trait concerning the presence of an enzyme thus bears a relationship to behavioral innovations. Moreover, you should see a feedback situation develop in which dairying decreases lactase deficiency, which increases milk toleration, which makes dairying more important as a food supply, which increases the selective pressure against individuals unable to digest milk.

Variation with hemoglobin provides a classic example of biocultural interaction. Hemoglobin is a giant protein which is found within the red blood cells. Its physiological function is to loosely combine with oxygen and transport the oxygen to each cell within the body.

Hemoglobins are not the same. They differ in molecular structure between different species, and often between individuals. Two variants of particular interest are type A (Hb A) and S (Hb S). The former is the kind which most adults have, while the frequency of the second is associated with the distribution of malaria.

This disease is perhaps the most common major infection in the world. It is transmitted to humans by mosquitos of the genus *Anopheles*. Infected mosquitos carry the one-celled *Plasmodium* parasites which are responsible. Hemoglobin S does not provide the parasite with the most suitable environment for its life cycle, and therefore individuals with Hb S have some protection.

The protection against malaria is not without its price. Homozygous Hb S genotypes usually suffer death at an early age from sickle-cell anemia. This is a hereditary disease in which the red blood cells have a distorted shape and are not readily able to pass through the tiny capillaries. They break apart within the blood stream more than they should and release free hemoglobin. This results in numerous clinical disorders, among which kidney failure is a common immediate cause of death. Death normally happens before the individual reaches the age of reproduction. Heterozygous genotypes lack the anemia but do have the malarial protection and will transmit the sickle-cell allele to following generations. Homozygous Hb A genotypes do not transmit the allele, but also lack the malarial protection which it provides.

The highest frequencies of the allele for Hb S are found in Africa, where it approaches 40% among some populations. One reason behind such a relatively high frequency is the spread of horticulture to the African rain forest.

How? The effects of humans on the ecosystem have consequences beyond their intention. Mosquito larvae require sunshine for their development, while an undisturbed rain forest is shady. As the invention of horticulture spread, clearings were cut and burned for the growing of crops. Such clearings offer an abundance of sunny pools of stagnant water, greater numbers of mosquitos, a higher prevalance of malaria, and a response by natural selection to increase the frequency of hemoglobin S and increase the number of people who die from sickle-cell disease.

One pessimistic (but realistic) point of view is that there is a price for everything.

MEASURING THE VARIATION

The goal of anthropology is to explain human variation. There are three steps in the process. The first is with its discovery. The second is assessment of its magnitude. The third is relating it to a general theory. For example, some people have blue eyes and some have brown. The discovery is a matter of simple observation. Assessing the magnitude requires quantifying the distribution. Scientists are crazy about numbers and for a good reason: determining the extent of the variability is the basis for testing theories about its cause. If, for example, one knows the frequency and dispersion of variation in eye color among different groups and compared it to environmental conditions, it is then possible to evaluate the empiric evidence with the ecological factors associated with it.

Merely being aware that biology, culture, and environment interact still leaves a curiosity in regard to the degree of association. This can only be satisfied with some kind of numerical analysis. We therefore interrupt the narrative to provide a primer on measurement.

There are two essential summaries for any set of data: central tendency and dispersion. Various descriptive statistics have been devised for each.

Central tendency describes an average. Common statistics for it include the mean, mode, and median. Examine the set of numbers below:

$$5-1-3-2-2-4-2-4-6$$

The mode is the most frequent number in a set. In this case, it is 2, since that number occurs most often. Modal statements form the bulk of social science writing. If an ethnographer states, for instance, that Apache men avoid their mothers-in-law, the meaning is that this is only the most frequent pattern of behavior.

The median is the number in the middle. More precisely, 50% of the values in the set exceed it and 50% are lower. To ascertain the median, rank the set in order and count.

$$
\left.
\begin{array}{l}
6 \\
5 \\
4 \\
4
\end{array}
\right\} \text{4 above}
$$

$$3 \text{————median}$$

$$
\left.
\begin{array}{l}
2 \\
2 \\
2 \\
1
\end{array}
\right\} \text{4 below}
$$

The median for the case above is 3. It is frequently used when a set has some extreme values, since the median is little influenced by the extremes.

The mean is the most commonly reported central tendency. To obtain it, add all the numbers together and divide by the number of cases.

$$\bar{x} = \Sigma/N$$

Don't pass the symbols by. The Σ symbol is the capital Greek letter sigma, and it tells you to add the numbers in the series. N represents the total number of observations. It is equal to nine observations for the data given. The symbol $\bar{x}$ (x bar) is an arbitrary designation for the mean. Thus:

$$
\begin{array}{l}
6 \\
5 \\
4 \\
4 \\
3 \\
2 \\
2 \\
2 \\
\underline{1} \\
\end{array}
$$

$$\Sigma = 29 \quad N = 9$$
$$\bar{x} = 29/9 = 3.22$$

The mean is a basic unit for comparing the difference between groups in regard to some typical characteristic.

It is just as important to recognize difference in dispersion—how heterogeneous one group is compared to another. Two populations could have, for example, the same mean, and yet one could be far more variable than the other. Central tendency alone contains less information than is desirable to know.

Examine the monthly precipitation charts for Portland, Oregon, and Tulsa, Oklahoma, in figure 9.3.

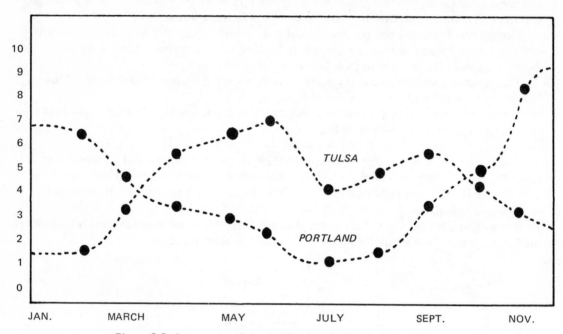

Figure 9.3. Average precipitation (inches) in Portland and Tulsa.

The mean annual precipitation between the two cities is about the same. Moreover, both chambers of commerce describe their climate as mild and pleasantly refreshing. Yet the pattern of rainfall is more variable. In Tulsa, the rain is heavy during the spring, and it usually comes from intense storms of short duration and in torrents of water. Portland, on the other hand, has rainy winters with long periods of drizzle. The difference in overall climatic pattern between the two cities is greater than the lesser difference between annual precipitation would indicate. The point is that a more complete understanding of a class of phenomena is enhanced by also investigating the variation within it.

The fundamental measurement of in-group heterogeneity is variance. The formula is

$$\sigma^2 = \frac{\Sigma d^2}{N-1}$$

The symbol d represents the deviation from the mean of each of the observations. The symbol σ is the small case Greek letter sigma in contrast to the upper case Σ for summation.

Notice the following sets:

A	B
2	1
2	3
2	4
2	0

The summation of both set A and set B is 8. (Add them both.) The mean of both sets is 2. (Divide the sum by the number of cases.) Observe, however, that they differ in heterogeneity; A has no variation, while B has variation. Variance gives us a standard measurement of the variability it contains.

To illustrate the calculation, let us take set B.

1. List the data in a column. Label it as x.
2. Calculate the mean of x. This is 2.
3. Find the difference between the mean of x and each observation.
4. Square each of the differences.
5. Add the total of the numbers you obtain.

Organizing the data into a table like the following is recommended.

x	$\bar{x}$	d	d^2
1	2	1	1
3	2	1	1
4	2	2	4
0	2	2	4
$\Sigma = 8$			$\Sigma = 10$
$\bar{x} = 2$			

6. Now refer to the formula and substitute.

$$\sigma^2 = \frac{10}{3}$$
$$\sigma^2 = 3.33$$

The higher the number obtained, the greater the amount of variation around the mean of the sample.

Practice. Calculate the variance for 2–1–3–0–2–4.

x	$\bar{x}$	d	d^2
2			
1			
3			
0			
2			
4			

$\Sigma =$

$\bar{x} =$

$\sigma^2 = \qquad \div$

$\sigma^2 =$

The answer is at the end of the chapter.

Another statistic (the standard deviation) is often used instead of the variance. Recall that we mentioned it in regard to radiocarbon dates in chapter 2. To calculate the standard deviation, simply take the square root of the variance you have already obtained.

$$\sigma = \sqrt{\sigma^2}$$

The standard deviation is the square root of the variance, and the variance is the standard deviation squared.

BIOLOGICAL VARIATION AND CULTURAL EVOLUTION

All organisms are affected by their environment. Likewise, all influence their environment in return. The human species does so to a degree unparalleled in nature. The man-made changes in our planet are so extensive that it is doubtful that any place on the globe (however remote) would lack some indication of the human presence. The reason for this is a platitude: cultural evolution provides a technology which can be taught by one person to another. Organic evolution is a naturally slow process compared to cultural change.

We want to finish with a consideration of how this circumstance bears a systematic and general consequence on human biological variation. For that, we need the concept of variance which you have just mastered.

First, a few words about culture in greater detail. It is often convenient to recognize three components: the technological, sociological, and ideological.

Ideology is the belief and value system of a people—their ideas of good and bad, right and wrong, the trivial and the important. While it is clear that ideology changes over time, it is a different matter to establish any general evolutionary scheme for it. The major problem is that direct evidence exists only in the form of oral or written tradition. Its interpretation is difficult. Furthermore, nothing can be traced more than a few thousand years at most. Possibly our remote ancestors had a less mechanistic world view than that of contemporary times. They probably recognized a multiplicity of animistic spirits. They may have been more in awe of natural phenomena. The integrity of the small group must surely have been a prime moral concern. All of these, however, are speculations based upon ethnographic analogy.

Sociological sphere refers to how a group is structured to stay together. Examples include kinship patterns, ritual institutions, methods of economic organization, divisions of labor, and many others.

The main evolutionary trend in this part of culture is generally agreed upon. It is a change from band to tribe to chiefdom to state.

The social organization of actual societies may be intermediate for any of these categories. We shall, however, briefly describe them as idealized levels. As such, they are depicted in figure 9.4.

A band to an anthropologist is not just any kind of small group. It is a particular way in which only the most primitive societies are organized. Population size within the band is low, as is the overall density. Subsistence is provided by hunting and gathering. Relationships between individuals are egalitarian. There are no full-time professionals. The daily activities do not differ much by sex and age from one individual to the next.

Tribes have mechanisms for integrating two or more bands. Such institutions are technically called *sodalities*. A sodality is any kind of integration not due simply to commonality of residence. Clans, age grades, and military societies, for instance, all serve to crosscut bands and unite the members of various bands into some mutual identification. Horticulture or hunting and gathering are the typical means of subsistence. Like bands, the geographical units are largely self-sufficient, and the population size and density remain fairly low.

As one might expect, chiefdoms have chiefs. Social grades of ranked order begin to appear, such as nobility, commoners, and slaves. There are full-time professionals, such as artisans, rulers, and priests. Relationships between individuals, groups, and geographical units become progressively more unequal. A centralized redistribution center receives goods, services, and labor.

States are even more complexly organized. Population size may number in the millions, and all modern states are dependent on agriculture for subsistence. Many anthropologists regard states and civilizations as virtually synonymous; that is, they have all the characteristics (such as writing and cities) mentioned in chapter 7. Modern states are also empires; a number of different ethnic groups are under a common political control. The United States, for example, contains groups of people originally from all over the world.

The technological component of culture does not refer only to modern inventions. It includes everything made by humans and the knowledge of how to do it. A chopping tool from the Lower Paleolithic is as much a technological product as is a cyclotron. They differ in complexity, but not in being culturally made devices.

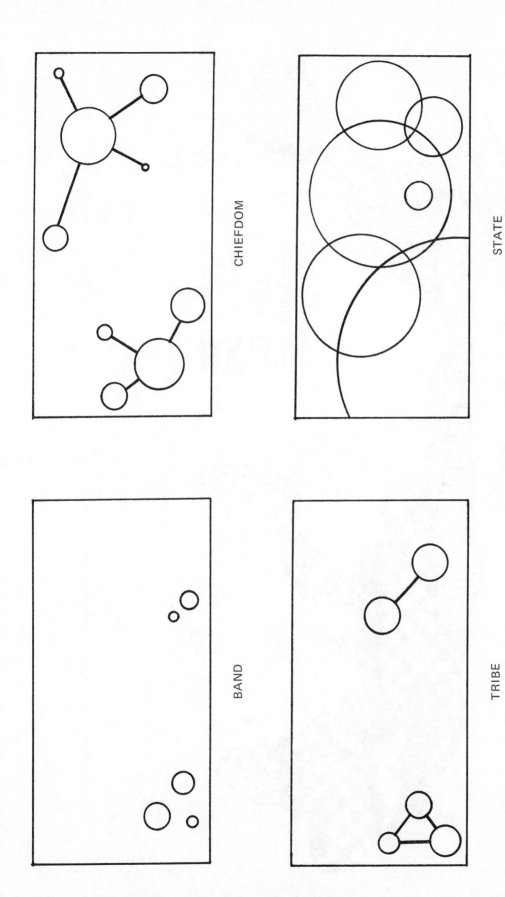

Figure 9.4. Population structure for bands, tribes, chiefdoms, and states.

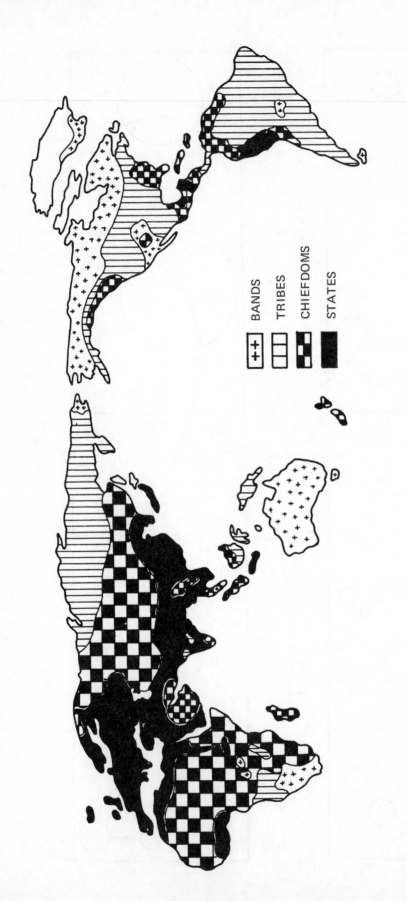

Figure 9.5. Generalized distribution of bands, tribes, chiefdoms, and states in the ethnographic present. After Beals and Kelso (1975).

BANDS

TRIBES

CHIEFDOMS

STATES

The overall course of technological evolution is well known; the rate of change has been increasing by geometric proportion, just as the increase in human population size has. Little change in tool types occurred at first. A 2-million-year-old hand axe differs only slightly from one made a million years later. Compare this to the rate of innovation in mechanical and electronic machines in your own lifetime. The amount of available energy per capita is a striking case in point. Our remote ancestors were limited to the energy produced by their own muscles. The use of fire, domestication of draft animals, application of the sail, and finally the industrial revolution created an increasing capacity for work—at least as meant by physicists. The exponential growth rate in technology and population is now so rapid that it is socially disturbing. It has possibly outstripped the capacity of our ideological and sociological ability to cope with it.

Some consequences for biological evolution from cultural evolution should be obvious. For example, consider how different the array of biological frequencies within the two American continents are today as compared to only 500 years ago. In 1478, the phenotypic and genotypic frequencies would be those of American Indians. Today they are a composite of world migration. The amount of change is at least a hundredfold compared to the ordinary slow process of natural selection. The difference is a result of cultural inventions which have greatly increased the mobility of individuals.

Five million years ago, our ancestors lived in small bands confined to parts of Africa. As culture evolved, groups were able to occupy more variable environments. They culturally and biologically adapted to a greater diversity. Since the adaptive requirements varied, this created an increased diversity for both biological and cultural traits. At the same time, the amount of isolation between groups would be great.

As the process continued, however, cultural innovations diminished the isolation between groups. The result is increasing biological and cultural variance within groups and decreasing that between them.

Empiric studies of this interaction have just begun. In the first attempt to measure the amount of association, variations in zygosity for three blood groups' genes were correlated with societies ranging from bands, tribes, chiefdoms, and states. In accordance with the theory, it was discovered that the average variability (as measured by heterozygosity) did increase as culture evolved. Likewise, the variance between groups diminished. It indicated that peoples of recent band organization averaged about 12% greater homogeneity than those found in state societies. Our fossil ancestors probably lived in even more homogeneous groups but with greater variation from one to the next. Theoretically, the same circumstance should apply to cultural and biological traits in general.

For our species as a whole, some of the major trends of biocultural evolution are these:

1. Groups occupied an increasing diversity of environments. In the process of adaption, the variance between groups increased.
2. The social integration of groups became more complex, evolving from bands to tribes to chiefdoms to states.
3. The rate of change in technology and population size increased geometrically.
4. Isolation between groups diminished, and as a result variance between groups diminished and variance within groups increased.
5. The total amount of human variation became constantly greater.

New combinations of experience, ideas, and genes were thus increasingly added to the structure of our existence. It is both the product and challenge of our evolutionary journey through the eons of time.

EXERCISE: APPLYING THE STANDARD DEVIATION

To illustrate how the idea of variation can be applied to the past, we suggest an exercise in which a series of modern specimens is compared to a fossil specimen whose identity is unknown. Before proceeding, however, it is necessary to discuss the standard deviation in regard to a normal curve.

Traits which are determined by a number of factors operating together generally form a characteristic graph known as a normal curve. Most of the observations will cluster around the mean, while extremes in either direction are more rare. Observe the distribution of stature in the classroom. Most individuals will be between 5 feet 2 inches and 6 feet 2 inches. Only a few people will be shorter or taller. If we were to plot the distribution, it would approximate the shape shown.

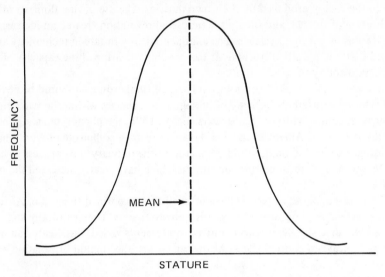

A standard deviation can be used to tell us how far from the mean a particular observation is expected to be a certain percent of the time. For this, we require a table of areas of the normal curve. An abbreviated version is shown.

Table of Areas of a Normal Curve

DISTANCE FROM MEAN ÷ STANDARD DEVIATION	PERCENT INCLUDED (ONE SIDE)	PERCENT INCLUDED (BOTH SIDES)
0.1	3.98	7.96
0.5	19.15	38.30
1.0	34.13	68.26
1.5	43.32	86.64
2.0	47.73	95.46
3.0	49.87	99.74
4.0	49.99	99.98

From Arkin and Colton (1963)

To demonstrate the use of the table, let us take a case in which the mean of a set of observations is 22.7 and the standard deviation is 0.8. Let us now take an observation having a value of 23.1. Assuming that the observation belongs to the same population, what is the probability of obtaining a value of 23.1 on the basis of chance alone?

1.   First, determine how far the observation is from the mean. (In this case, it is 0.4 units.)
2.   Divide the distance from the mean by the standard deviation. (0.4/0.8 = .5.)

It is thus one-half of one standard deviation from the mean. Check the table for the area included for this value. Observe that it is 38.30%. The probability of obtaining a deviation from the mean as great as this, or greater than this, is therefore 61.70% (subtract from 100%). Conversely, we can expect to find a case closer to the mean only 38.30% of the time. Therefore, we would expect this to happen about 6 times out of 10 occurrences, and chance alone could easily account for the event. If the value were to be 5 standard deviations from the mean, this would be expected to happen less than .01% of the time, and the sample probably represents a different population.

Note that the further from the mean that a sample occurs, the less likely it is. A person with a stature of 6 feet 5 inches or 4 feet 8 inches is, for instance, much more likely to be found than one being 7 feet 5 inches or 3 feet 4 inches. For this chapter, we will consider any sample which is greater than two standard deviations from the mean as being statistically significant. This is an arbitrary decision which any researcher must make: deciding upon some level of significance. For most scientific work, it corresponds to a probability of less than 5%.

Your practical exercise is this. You will be given a series of modern human mandibles and a fossil specimen which is unidentified. Let us bestow upon it the name from chapter 1: *Alphonsopithecus.* Observe that the mandible is rather large and massive. What we wish to determine is whether or not, in respect to size at least, it appears to fit within the range of variation of modern man. If not, perhaps it belongs to a different species.

As one test, we may compare the maximum width of the mandible.

1. Examine the fossil cast. Measure the maximum width of the mandible with sliding calipers. Measure from a point directly behind the second premolar.
2. Do the same for a series of 10 mandibles from modern humans. Each of these should be labeled with numbers. Record the value for each.
3. Calculate the mean and standard deviation for the modern series.
4. What is the value for *Alphonsopithecus?* How many standard deviations is it from the mean for the modern series?
5. About how many times would you expect a deviation as great as this to occur by accident?
6. Do you believe, on the basis of what you have done, that *Alphonsopithecus* represents a modern human? Is it more likely to belong to a different category?

Your analysis of the fossil could, of course, be more sophisticated and comprehensive. On the other hand, the basic ideas and techniques are the same as those actually used by paleontologists, and by researchers in general.

Answer to the problem on page 103:

x	$\bar{x}$	d	d^2
2	2	0	0
1	2	1	1
3	2	1	1
0	2	2	4
2	2	0	0
4	2	2	4
$\Sigma = \overline{12}$			$\Sigma = \overline{10}$
$\bar{x} = 2$			

$$\sigma^2 = \frac{\Sigma d^2}{N-1}$$

$$= \frac{10}{5}$$

$$= 2$$

Appendix

SUGGESTED TEACHING AIDS

Chapter 1

    Monkeys, Apes and Man (Films, Inc., 50 min., color)

    Survey of the Primates (Appleton-Century-Crofts, 38 min., color)

    The film *Monkeys, Apes, and Man* is 50 minutes long. It is an excellent and entertaining movie on primate behavior. *Survey of the Primates* is slightly shorter; it reviews most of the workbook material. The best audiovisual supplement is a trip to the local zoo.

    Actual primate skeletons are more realistic than drawings for the exercise on locomotion. They are available from Carolina Biological Supply. Anthropometric equipment can be obtained from Siber-Hegner. Instructor demonstration of the types of locomotion invariably provides amusement and perhaps some education as well. If space and facilities are available, why not have a Primate Olympics? We have given Awards of the Golden Banana to the winners of the various events. Competition in the bipedal walk and quadrupedalism (the tree shrew shuffle) is fairly safe. The knuckle race and gibbon glide (brachiation) should not be tried without special safety equipment.

Chapter 2

    How Old Is Old? (Time-Life, 29 min., color)

    The recommended commercial presentation is *How Old Is Old?* It concentrates on methods of absolute dating and is about 30 minutes long.

    The most practical classroom addition is counting tree rings and matching an overlapping sequence.

Chapter 3

    Calculators will be appreciated for chapters 3, 7, and 9.

Chapter 4

    Early Stone Tools (Penn State, 28 min., color)

    Demonstration is an easy substitute for the exercise on making a tool. You can find suitable stone with the help of a geology department.

Chapter 5

    The Man Hunters (Films, Inc., 52 min., color)

    The fossil casts specifically mentioned are Sterkfontein 5, Swartkrans 48, and *H. erectus,* adult female, Choukoutien. Sources for casts include Carolina Biological Supply, the Wenner-Gren Foundation, and the University of Pennsylvania Museum. Fragmentary and nonhominid specimens make the exercise more interesting. Actual skulls are preferable to pictures. Sources include Carolina and Wards. Having a skeletal variety of age and sex is ideal.

Chapter 6

    4-Butte-1 (U. of Calif. Ext. Media Center, 33 min., color)

    Gatecliffe: American Indian Rock Shelter (National Geographic, 24 min., color)

    The Early American (Shell Films, 41 min., color)

    We recommend supplementing the unit with a discussion of the local archaeology and ethnology.

Chapter 7

    Lost World of the Maya (Time-Life, 60 min. color)

Gerald Brush has written a conversational program (*Maya*) specifically designed for an introduction to the use of computers. It is a Mayan calendar converter for OS-3 systems and may be obtained by writing to the authors.

Chapter 8

The Incredible Machine (National Geographic, 60 min., color)

Either videotapes or personal demonstration will provide help in performing the exercises. *The Incredible Machine* contains some remarkable photography to show the operation of the human body.

Pseudoisochromatic plates are available from the American Optical Co. A number of biological supply houses (Carolina, Scientific Products, VWR) offer blood typing antisera. Solutions of PTC in squeeze bottles are preferable to impregnated papers. Instructions for preparing solutions of PTC may be found in Montagu (1960:584).

Chapter 9

Yanomamö: A Multidisciplinary Study (National Audiovisual Center, 43 min., color)

Yanomamö demonstrates a cooperative field investigation.

One simple laboratory supplement is the phosphate solubility test for the presence of hemoglobin S. Kits can be obtained from Carolina. Preparing a karyotype requires more extensive equipment. Write to Hyland. The mandible fragment originally identified as *Meganthropus paleojavanicus* (from the University of Pennsylvania Museum) is an inexpensive and excellent choice to represent *Alphonsopithecus ridiculous*. It is preferable for the students to take the measurements themselves. If not, the following is a comparison with 10 modern mandibles taken at random.

A. ridiculous	Modern Series	
3.2	2.1	2.1
	2.0	1.4
	1.9	1.6
	2.4	1.5
	1.7	1.6

DISTRIBUTORS

Answers to the problems, examination questions, and the program for *Maya* are available from K. Beals, Dept. of Anthropology, Oregon State University, Corvallis, OR 97331.

Equipment

American Optical, Buffalo, NY 14215
Carolina Biological Supply, Burlington, NC 27215
Hyland Division of Travenol Laboratories, 4501 Colorado Blvd., Los Angeles, CA 90039
Scientific Products, 1430 Waukegan Rd., McGaw Park, IL 60085
Siber-Hegner, 8 W. 30th St., New York, NY 10001
Turtox/Cambosco, 8200 S. Hoyne Ave., Chicago, IL 60620
University Museum, 33rd and Spruce St., Philadelphia, PA 19104
VWR Scientific, P.O. Box 10287, Portland, OR 97210
Wards's Natural Science Establishment, P.O. Box 1749, Monterey, CA 93940
Wenner-Gren Foundation, 14 E. 71st St., New York, NY 10021

Audiovisual Material

Appleton-Century-Crofts, 440 Park Ave. S., New York, NY 10016
California University Extension Media Center, 2223 Fulton St., Berkeley, CA 94720
Films, Inc., 144 Wilmette Ave., Wilmette, IL 60091

National Audiovisual Center, National Archives and Records Services, Washington, D.C. 40409
National Geographic, P.O. Box 1640, Washington, D.C. 20013
Pennsylvania State University Audio-Visual Aid Library, University Park, PA 16802
Shell Film Library, 1433 Sadlier Circ., W. Dr., Indianapolis, IN 46239
Time-Life, 100 Eisenhower Dr., Paramus, NJ 07652

References Cited

Arkin, Herbert, and Raymond R. Colton
    1963   Tables for Statisticians. 2nd ed. New York: Barnes & Noble.
Beals, Kenneth L., and A. J. Kelso
    1975   Genetic Variation and Cultural Evolution. American Anthropologist 77:566-79.
Brace, C. Loring, Harry Nelson, and Noel Korn
    1971   Atlas of Fossil Man. New York: Holt, Rinehart & Winston.
Braidwood, Robert J.
    1967   Prehistoric Men. 7th ed. Glenview, Ill.: Scott Foresman.
Chard, Chester S.
    1975   Man in Prehistory. New York: McGraw-Hill.
Clark, Grahame
    1967   The Stone Age Hunters. New York: McGraw-Hill.
Clark, W. E. Le Gros
    1964   The Fossil Evidence for Human Evolution. 2nd ed. Chicago: University of Chicago Press.
Jennings, Jesse D.
    1974   Prehistory of North America. 2nd ed. New York: McGraw-Hill.
Kelso, A. J.
    1974   Physical Anthropology. 2nd ed. Philadelphia: Lippincott.
Montagu, M. F. Ashley
    1960   An Introduction to Physical Anthropology. 3rd ed. Springfield, Ill.: Charles C. Thomas.
Movius, H. L., Jr.
    1956   The Old Stone Age. *In* Man, Culture, and Society. Harry Shapiro, ed. New York: Oxford.
Thompson, J. Eric
    1954   The Rise and Fall of Maya Civilization. Norman, Oklahoma: University of Oklahoma Press.
Tunnell, Gary G.
    1973   Culture and Biology. Minneapolis: Burgess.